FROM STONE
TO LIVING
WORD

FROM STONE
TO LIVING
WORD

letting the BIBLE live again

DEBBIE BLUE

BrazosPress

Grand Rapids, Michigan

© 2008 by Debbie Blue

Published by Brazos Press
a division of Baker Publishing Group
P.O. Box 6287, Grand Rapids, MI 49516-6287
www.brazospress.com

Printed in the United States of America

Library of Congress Cataloging-in-Publication Data
Blue, Debbie.
    From stone to living word : letting the Bible live again / Debbie Blue.
        p. cm.
    Includes bibliographical references.
    ISBN 978-1-58743-190-6 (pbk.)
    1. Bible—Criticism, interpretation, etc. I. Title.
BS511.3.B63 2008
220.6—dc22   2007029555

Contents

PART ONE: **Making Stones**

1. Nooses and Knots   9
2. Ancient Riddles   33

PART TWO: **Reviving the Dead**
Marrow

3. In the Beginning   63
4. The Original Lie   69
5. A Midrash on the Tower of Babel   79
6. God's Mouth on Our Nostrils   87
7. Two Mule-Loads of Dirt   95

Flesh

8. The Ultimate Anti-Idolatry Story   107
9. The Mother of God   117
10. A Pathological Attraction to Revolutionaries   123
11. Look at How You Hear   133
12. How to Entangle Him in His Talk   141
13. Tip the Boat Over   151

5

Blood

14. Drinking to the Dregs   161
15. Murdering God   171
16. Everlasting Life   189
17. Reverse Glory   197

Epilogue: **Food**

18. Delight in the Fatness and Live   209

Notes   217

PART ONE

MAKING
STONES

1

Nooses and Knots

I'm not good with answers. I used to do okay with them on tests in school, but lately someone asks, "How do you get to 35E?" and I can't remember any street names or which way is east. The other day when I was getting my hair cut, a woman asked me where I lived and all I could do was point. I did manage, in the end, "By the river." She looked at me like I was two and said, "That's nice."

When someone from my church says they'd like to arrange a time to get together because they have some questions, I tend to get a little panicky. I love it when people want to get together to talk. I like having coffee with people and listening to them put their lives into words. I'm amazed at lives. They are heartbreaking and outrageous and beautiful and sad. It's when I get the feeling that people might need me to do more than listen—need me to offer guidance—that I feel the possibility of clarity vanish, the ambiguity of every situation rushes in. This is admittedly not a good quality for a church leader.

The word *pastor* derives from sheepherder, animal husbandry. *Herd* seems different from *lead*, less gallant. Last summer my kids and I went to the Minnesota Sheep and Wool Festival. It was in Mora, a small town about half an hour from our farm. We saw lots of shepherds there. Some wore dirty jeans and coughed and spit. Some had beer bellies. A young couple who looked more urban than rural was selling cheese. Sheep's cheese. They milked their flocks and then laced the product with fennel and rosemary. I wonder if shepherds ever really watched their flocks or if they sat in the shade playing cards or the lute or smoking and drinking. Did shepherds really lead the sheep, or was it more like they followed them around, yelling out occasionally to try to scare away coyotes? I don't know that much about shepherds. I don't know if *pastor* is a very good word for what preachers do. I'm certainly startled when someone addresses me as Pastor Blue. It seems funny to me. Not just funny weird, but it makes me want to laugh funny. Not at them, but just the whole idea.

It seems like the church has a reputation for being a place you go for answers, or to get your life straightened out. That's probably a lot because the church has encouraged this image of itself. Some churches promise this on billboards or cable TV: Are you messed up? Is your life in shambles? Jesus can make a difference in your life right now, this minute. A smiling man vows that his church is committed to helping every person, regardless of background and economic status, to achieve his or her fullest potential. He seems comfortable, as if he belongs in the TV studio with his nicely fitting suit and open collar and his haircut and the bright lights and his perfect teeth. Call 1-800-555-5555. I wonder who is on the other end of the line and what they say. Maybe something wonderful and helpful. And there are testimonials. I grew up hearing constant testimonials from former drug addicts or atheist devil worshipers or gang members, stories of how people walked through the doorway of a church and from that moment on their lives got better, cleaner. I believe people can help people and churches can help people. Maybe these churches really do deliver what they advertise, but I can't help thinking it's a misrepresentation of what faith is like.

Often when I'm struggling to write a sermon, feeling more like a squirrel than a shepherd, I'll vaguely remember something Father Zossima said. So I scan the pages of *The Brothers Karamazov* looking for that sublime or searing something. It's usually around midnight, and I usually get a headache, and I usually don't find it, and I wish I could just sit down with him and ask him a few questions. I realize he's a character in a book, but I admire him. I like his style. Eduard Thurneysen describes Zossima's pastoral approach: "It is not designed to remove [people's] burdens, to lead them out of the uncertainties of their lives, but it is intended to lead [people] into them truly and for the first time, . . . for in persevering in the uncertainties of life, he sees the only way of redemption."[1]

I honestly don't know what it would even quite mean to straighten a life out. I have hardly ever seen anything alive that seemed very straight or very neat. I'm not sure if you can keep anything that is alive entirely clean. Being alive is just very wild. Nerve endings and eating and anger and orgasms. I've heard that the color you paint your bedroom can affect how you feel when you wake up in the morning, and so can clouds. Every moment it seems like you truly can and truly can't predict what will happen every next moment. I don't even know what dark matter and dark energy are, but apparently they are the dominant constituents of the universe. There's the warping and curving of time and space, extra space dimensions, quantum jitters. Uncertain is too mild a way of putting it—it's outrageous to be alive. Life isn't simple and coherent. It is inexplicable and lush and desperate and sad and beautiful and scary. I don't know how anyone could "figure it out." The factors are beyond figuring. It would be like stuffing sunflowers and giant sequoias and birth and death and ten thousand variables into an equation. And yet we all seem to be constantly trying.

People talk a lot about the necessity of stability: we must have stable homes, a stable environment for our children, stable personalities, stable marriages, stable jobs, as if stability were the highest good. But even though my family eats dinner together, though we have managed to establish a bedtime routine, though the kids generally brush their teeth at least two times a day, I don't feel like I encounter all that much that I could very accurately describe as quite "stable." What does stability really even look like?

I know what striving for the appearance of stability looks like, like me not wailing and pounding my chest (even though I feel like it) when my ten-year-old son says maybe this year he'd rather I didn't join him in the school cafeteria for Parent Lunch Day. Like my copastors walking into the sanctuary with what seems like perfect equanimity even though five seconds before church we were all snapping at each other and freaked out because there's no communion bread and the baptistery flooded and Jonathan's parents, who suspect us of being liberal pagan imposters, are in the front pew and Russell's preaching a sermon he entitled (perhaps a tad recklessly) "There is No Hell." Striving for the appearance of stability seems to involve being a little removed, to require some rational detachment.

12

People are always describing my husband as stable. I've even done it myself. When I first met him I thought he was some sort of Zen master. But I know him really well now, and I know that what appears to be peaceful steadiness is often anxiety, fear, and repression. I like him a lot, probably better than anyone else; I've just realized he's not quite Buddha. And actually Zen masters aren't really all that into the appearance of stability. Huston Smith says,

> Entering the Zen outlook is like stepping through Alice's looking glass. One finds oneself in a topsy-turvy wonderland in which everything seems quite mad—charmingly mad for the most part but mad all the same. It is a world of bewildering dialogues, obscure conundrums, stunning paradoxes, flagrant contradictions, and abrupt non sequiturs, all carried off in the most urbane, cheerful, and innocent style. . . . Its uniqueness [lies] in the fact that it is so concerned with the limitations of language and reason that it makes their transcendence the central intent of its method.[2]

Maybe when we long for stability, straightening, figuring, we are longing for something a bit more inert than life, which is sometimes unbearably ert—tempestuous and unruly. We hold jobs and stay together but fights break out, something in our brain chemistry undoes us, the foundation collapses. Cells are multiplying riotously in my friend's body, growing an aberrant mass that may kill her. Life seems more like uncontrollable streams all intertwined than bedrock.

It's no wonder that the church wants to lend a hand, help solve the equation, promise people a nice and solid firm foundation. That's what we often desperately believe we need. Much of the Christian enterprise is devoted to trying to provide this. But maybe it's not really an unshakable infrastructure, solid conclusions, or tidiness that we need. And faith isn't actually something that supplies us with immovable ground.

"Faith is not, therefore, a standing, but a being suspended and hanging without ground under our feet" (Karl Barth).[3] "Faith begins only there where in the confirmations and concepts, confirmation and concept cease, all assurances and certainty end" (Eduard Thurneysen).[4] "If any one imagines that he knows something, he does not yet know as he ought to know" (Paul: 1 Corinthians 8:2).

Striving for certainty or the appearance of stability may have more to do with fear of all sorts of things—societal disapproval, impermanence, messiness, life—than with anything very true, or very honest, or even terribly crucial or highly good. It might be more of a cutting off, or a taming, or even a deceit at some level, than a revealing. Nietzsche said, "I call a lie: wanting *not* to see something one does see, wanting not to see something *as* one sees it."[5] The church seems often to get involved in that lie a little, as if everything would be better if we could just pretend that reality, life, the world, were less complicated. If we could just rein it all in or come up with a system to explain it simply or pour concrete over steel girders, make believe it can or should be coherent and comprehensible, that would be the solution to life. And maybe we have to do quite a bit of pretending just to get ourselves to go out and make money and obey traffic laws and get our kids to school on time. But life really isn't simple. And I'm sorry if this is not good for the children, if we really cannot provide them with a stable environment. But then again, I'm not. I'm happy they are alive, and I have some inkling of what that might mean: all sorts of raging things.

The clarity of idolatry

I think a lot of what we call faith is actually idolatry. Life is beyond our control, and that's not necessarily what we're after: unruly and uncontrollable life. A solid rock may sound more appealing. The church I grew up in loved the rock rhetoric. It was in the hymnbooks and promotional materials and every sermon. The pastor praised God that we did not have to suffer the shifting sands, children sang about the solid rock on which they stood, teenagers prayed that there would be no waves to knock them off. We were rock people. Life was not full of contradictions, or if it seemed to be, they were only apparent. Bible Baptist Church assured us that we had an absolute, rock hard, unchanging, and perfectly coherent foundation. They also talked a lot about needing to have a personal relationship with Jesus, but though they said "relationship" plenty, this seemed to involve strapping our feet to a boulder more than actually living in a relationship with a God who was truly alive.

Nietzsche accused theologians and philosophers and the church of killing and stuffing whatever they worshiped. He said we threaten the life of what we revere.[6] Maybe it's because the life itself seems threatening.

The church has always confessed that our concepts of God and our language about God can't adequately express or contain God. And this isn't considered a shortcoming or cause to despair; God is incomprehensibly marvelous, matchless, wonderful. I doubt you could find a church that would say otherwise, and yet we also seem to be, honestly, uncomfortable with the incomprehensibly marvelous. We want to comprehend. I certainly do. I desperately love to comprehend. I want to comprehend fully. Everybody and everything all around me all the time. I'm impatient with hiddenness. I want to feel like I have a handle on something. But in order to grasp something, to comprehend it, you have to be able to nail it down a little, fix it in your gaze. If it moves, it gets away, it blurs.

Jean-Luc Marion defines idolatry as "the subjection of the divine to the human condition for experience of the divine." We want the divine available to us. Of course we do, but in order to make it available we "freeze its face." Obviously, for us Protestants, it's not so much in a statue. Bible Baptist didn't have any actual rocks in its vestibule with God's features carved into them, but we had metaphorical rocks up the wazoo. We had concepts and images and ideas and dogmas about God that were hard and fast and in no way open to negotiation. We wanted to be assured of God's presence in these concepts, but "by establishing such an availability of the divine within the fixed, if not frozen face," we "deceitfully but radically eliminate the lofty irruption and undeniable alterity that properly attest the divine. . . . The idol makes the divine available, secures it, and in the end distorts it. Its culmination mortally finishes the divine."[7] Reducing the unfathomably gracious, infinitely loving, sweet sublime to something we can grasp is the move of idolatry.

I like to think I'm not a controlling person. I don't want to control anybody or anything—I just want to comprehend them or it. But I can see how controlling and comprehending might be related. If knowing means "grasping," well, that puts it in your hands. Nietzsche thought our attempts to understand truth are often more about mastering and controlling it than illuminating it. And they often reduce it more than reveal it. It's not surprising to me that we tend toward idolatry. Who doesn't want something that can be grasped, to get a handle on things, to get a rope around it and pull it in? It's almost like we have idolatry in our

16

DNA, like we just can't stand to live with something we can't grasp or have some control over, so we fix it, freeze it, pin it down. We get out our rope and lasso and knot and noose until we're pulling on the rope so hard that what may have been at first "bedazzling"[8] can now be mounted on our wall, more like a neat little package or a stuffed bird than an incomprehensibly wonderful Other. It's no wonder we are relentless idol makers, but it might be better if we didn't call our idolatry *faith*.

Life, for most of us, is not full of clear paths and voices from heaven. Idols help to make up for that deficiency. Life is outrageous. Idols help us know how to proceed. So we form and fashion ideas, beliefs, rules to live by, ways of life, cultural codes. Idols are understandings we cling to that end up taking the place of God. This isn't always an overtly religious project. Some have claimed that the entire Western philosophical tradition is idolatrous.[9] Idols are concepts and ideas that come to rule the world, or your world. Capitalism or communism or self-help strategies or macrobiotics or punk rock. They help us choose our church, our mates, and what shoes we wear. They help us know what life is permissible or desirable and what life is not, whether we're suburbanites or urbanites or skinnyites or church ladies or revolutionaries. Idols provide us with goals. Idols might make us feel good about ourselves or they might make us feel bad about ourselves; they might tell us how we should look or how we should act or how everyone else should look and act. We probably have little gods by the thousands: The Ideal Body, The Ideal Man, The Good Christian. Idols can be very artistically and beautifully and brilliantly rendered. They can be therapeutic. They can be more or less sophisticated. They can be super smart and creative and sensible, or they can be a bit silly. Idols are the things we cling to (even if it's a clinging that renounces clinging) and bow down to that are not God. It is hard to imagine what the world would look like without idolatry. It is so prevalent. It is the way the world works.

The idolatry the Hebrew prophets were constantly up in arms about all over the Bible wasn't some senseless and perverse obsession with obviously ridiculous, made-up gods. It wasn't profane activity; it was pretty much the opposite. It was about giving a face to the divine, giving the mystery recognizable features. The people didn't (at least initially) believe that the faces they gave to the divine adequately contained the divine, but the faces they made gave them something clearer to look at. As a kid, I thought idolatry was what I saw in Cecil B. DeMille's film version of *The Ten Commandments*: people dancing madly around the golden calf, all dark and steamy; sweating, whirling bodies; people who were obviously senseless and maybe drugged or drunk or just recklessly sinful in a way I wasn't much afraid of being. But the Israelites weren't drawn away from Yahweh because they were drugged and senseless, but because they longed for the order and availability that burning incense and sacrificing in the "high places" seemed to promise.

At the beginning of each new year in Babylon, the much-denounced idolatrous Babylonians would reenact the creation of the world, the battle of Marduk the Creator and Tiamat the Sea Monster. Tiamat was the uncontrollable, raging chaos that everyone feared. He was the unknown, slithering through the depths of the raging sea. Tiamat was the force that constantly threatens to overflow its banks and destroy civilization, or eat up your children, or swallow whatever fragile stability you've managed to eke out for your life. Tiamat was the ultimate source of anxiety. So every year the Babylonians would reenact the monster's threatening, and every year the great Marduk would end up defeating it. All the scary out-of-controlness would dissolve into the water, the chaos monster would be defeated once more, and humanity would be rescued from the threatening wild. The whole thing seems kind of brilliant and beautiful. I want the ultimate source of anxiety to be defeated. I can see participating in a religion that promises security and tries to maintain order. I have done so. Admittedly the reenactment of the threatening chaos at the new year's festival in Babylon involved some things that we don't see in most of our churches: "erotic license, orgies and so on."[10] Occasionally it also involved human sacrifice. But that's not so different from what we do with our religions, is it? Lives must be sacrificed in the service of ideals. This is not an unusual thing to hear people say.

It probably wouldn't have been such a big deal to the prophets of Yahweh if the people of Israel were worshiping plain old, uninteresting, not very compelling rocks. But it wasn't like that. The people didn't think they were worshiping idols when they observed the rites of Baal or danced in front of Marduk; they believed they were doing what was necessary for life—to get food, or find meaning, or bring peace. Mircea Eliade, a religious historian (who was also probably a fascist), talks about these early rituals as a quest to take chaotic space and time and make it sacred. In order to do anything to live, he says, humanity needed to acquire "a fixed point." Without a fixed point, he says, orientation in the world would have seemed impossible.[11]

Altars and incense and rituals, bowing down to Marduk, helped to orient the people. It was a way to make life feel less out of control, to order the world. The idolatry that the Hebrew prophets railed against wasn't perverse and profane and senseless. It was profoundly religious. If occasionally there were rocks involved, that makes a lot of sense too. Rocks can be religiously significant in all sorts of ways. They don't change. They are solid and stable. They seem absolute and invulnerable and permanent. Rocks have attractive qualities. Idols aren't just stupid rocks that stupid people worship; they fulfill our longing for something we can grasp, comprehend, something solid we can fix in our gaze.

My Sri Lankan statue

Nell, who goes to my church, recently brought me a Buddha back from Sri Lanka. I love my Buddha. It's not a fat jolly one. It's black and sleek and serene, and it sparkles. I've been carrying it around with me, putting it on my desk when I write and by the sink when I'm making dinner for the kids or washing dishes. I panicked the other day when I couldn't find it. I feel like I'm going to forget to be peaceful without it. I like looking at it. It reminds me to be mindful and not to get irritated with my kids and to talk nicely. The kids are even on to it. When I did get a bit irritable the other night after Olivia drew on the kitchen table with a permanent green Sharpie, she said to me, "Mom, where's your Buddha?"

Nell gave it to me right before church began in a perfect little white box, and all through the service I couldn't resist opening the box and looking at it because it made me so happy. I was trying to be discreet about it, because I thought if Fred Hall sees me acting all in love with my Buddha, he will definitely have some questions for me, and I won't be good with the answers. Fred is a beautiful old pietistic Lutheran who loves Jesus and wants to like House of Mercy but worries when he thinks we stray from the path.

I was immediately attached to my Buddha. Clearly it is no portal for me into the riches of Buddhism, but I like the weight of it in my hand, and running my fingers over its surface. I like my relationship with my Buddha. It encourages me to be good and serene and control my anger. But it's not really much of a relationship. It's a rock. If it has any transforming qualities, it is because it reminds me of what I already know and what I want to remember. My rock Buddha is very comforting and reassuring and helpful. It helps me to feel oriented. It works. But perhaps it's something altogether different that I really need. I have a feeling that if I had a Zen master, he'd probably throw my Buddha on the ground and smash it to pieces, or dangle it from a fishing rod, or paint it with pink polka dots, something to baffle and bewilder.

Idols aid us, console us, and give us direction. Idolatry makes so much sense that it is surprising that there's such an enormous polemic against the whole enterprise in the Bible. But there really, really is. Scripture devotes an enormous amount of time and space trying to derail it. The Bible is relentlessly anti-idolatrous. And I don't think it's all out of some sort of prudish, narrow-minded, strait-laced, puritanical, rigid, pagan-hating disapproval of certain rituals. I think it's an astounding revelation that however much idolatry seems to secure life, it actually diminishes it. It doesn't make life, it takes it. It may provide stability and orientation, but it is giving our lives to what is not alive. Idolatry is death.

The Other (or the outrageousness of Christianity and love)

There's a weird thing about the Christian faith: faith. It's thoroughly dependent on the existence of an Other who is profoundly alive and always a little outside the sphere of what we know, dependent on something that is not in

21

our control, something definitely beyond our grasp, beyond grasping. Faith is more about depending on things unseen, things incomprehensible, than it is about making things sacred or ordering our world.

James Alison, a British theologian and Catholic priest, taught a class at our church about faith. I took about a thousand pages of notes. I'm not sure if this is word for word, but it might be (imagine it spoken slowly with a British accent). "Faith," he said, "is not an assent to a set of propositions, an assent to live according to some sort of principle or practice, even—it is a belief in an Other coming towards us and transforming us. It depends on the reliability of that Other. To have faith in God is very different from consenting to an ideology. It's not so much about what we do, but what the Other is doing to us, and how that affects who we are and what we do. It's a belief that we are undergoing something at the hands of an Other that enables us to live differently."

This may be weird and embarrassing and even slightly offensive (given what we usually believe is absolutely necessary for order or peace or to make the world better), but it is also pretty core. If core is even a word that works very well for an Other teeming with life.

There is a tension between faith and religion, one that you see played out over and over again throughout the Bible, with the prophets screaming that God doesn't want your sacrifices and burnt offerings. God wants your steadfast love (whatever that can possibly mean). And Jesus, battling with the Pharisees, the purveyors of religion, insists that everything hangs on this one thing: love God with all your heart and all your soul and all your mind, and love your neighbor as yourself (whatever that can possibly mean).

Faith is not ordering our lives according to principles we can firmly grasp, it's being transformed in ways we probably don't even have any idea we need to be, by a living Other who is always outside our grasp—a God who is profoundly, wildly, radically, maybe practically unbearably alive. And we are created, sustained, and redeemed by our relationship with the living God, not by our valiant and sometimes beautiful and sometimes violent and horrible attempts to make order or meaning or to control or comprehend. We are redeemed by the love of God. That is pretty much at the core of any orthodox Christianity. It is enormously important to faith, and it is a very wild claim: it's not the things (systems, ideologies, ideas) we are attached to that will give us life, save us, redeem us, but the love of the living God.

Love

It's hard to even talk about love without sounding corny and trite and sentimental and naive, without feeling just a little silly and romancey and young and like you don't know what you're talking about. Probably this is because we don't know what we're talking about most of the time when we talk about love. Maybe because love is not entirely comprehensible. But it seems like you can hardly hear the biblical witness or the historical witness of the church without hearing about love.

Bruce Benson, in his book *Graven Ideologies*, says, "Reflecting on our potential for idol creation can be an overwhelming and even frightening exercise. Not only are we capable of creating idols and worshiping them, we are likewise capable of being almost or completely blind to their existence."[12] He says idols are "subtle and elusive . . . constantly developing and shifting in identity. Just when we recognize them and take aim, they can take on a different form."[13] We can hardly speak about God without spitting out an idol every other second; sometimes it seems like we hardly know how to think or act without idols to guide us. Idols help us to order and categorize and calculate. Love, however, resists calculation, order, or category. Idols contain, while love, says Benson, "is profligate."[14]

This isn't a problem or shortcoming of love. Benson quotes Marion as saying, "Love does not suffer from the unthinkable or from the absence of conditions, but is reinforced by them."[15] In trying to imagine what might be outside of idolatry, some of the most erudite and untrite and un-naive thinkers come pretty close to talking about what I think we're talking about when we talk about love. Heidegger writes about "non-objectifying thinking" and "poetic thinking." Benson quotes Heidegger as saying, "Poetic thinking is being in the presence of . . . and for the god. Presence means: simple willingness that wills nothing, counts on no successful outcome."[16] Emmanuel Levinas speaks about "knowing otherwise than according to knowledge."[17] Marion speaks of a call that comes "from outside of me" and "displaces me as center of my world."[18] Whereas our systems are often founded on the notion that morality, justice, and right action are rationally calculable, Derrida recognizes that, though we must calculate, "justice escapes all calculation. . . . Choices, on Derrida's view, cannot be made in a mechanical, calculable, programmable way."[19]

Love isn't much like rock-hard certainty. A firm foundation doesn't even sound quite right. Love and relationship seem very different from order and coherence and simplicity. A loving relationship may be constant and enduring, never-ending, but even so, *stable* and *coherent* and *simple* are not words that describe it very well. Maybe there's not so much stability as we'd like. Maybe the foundation isn't quite as firm as we'd like. Maybe what holds us is love, and though it might not guarantee us security or control or comprehension, it is the most hopeful and transforming possibility.

Like a rolling stone

I feel sometimes like I love my idols—ideas that I see clearly, ideologies that seem brilliant to me, things I cling to in order to feel secure, my rock Buddha, my most precious constructs, and Bob Dylan. Maybe not so much now, but there was a time.

I'd been in Oregon for a year in the mountains surrounded by big trees and wild places, and I was preparing to head home to flat Indiana. Some boy I was into at the time, some boy with long hair and a VW van, recorded all his Dylan albums for me on cassette tapes so I might head to the domesticated Midwest with a voice of undomestication. The boy was very into Dylan and very into telling me everything he knew about him and convincing me of his genius. He piled books of interviews, books with pictures, books of lyrics on my front seat. All day I'd drive listening to the cassettes, and at night I'd lie on the scratchy sheets in the Motel Six or the Broken Spoke Inn with the doors double locked and read interviews.

When everyone was saying what a brilliant poet Dylan was, someone asked him if he thought of himself as primarily a poet. Dylan said, "No . . . the word doesn't mean any more than the word 'house.' There are people who write *poems* and people who write po*ems*. Other people write *poems*. . . . I don't call myself a poet because I don't like the word. I'm a trapeze artist."[20] He said, "Chaos is a friend of mine. It's like I accept him, does he accept me. Truth is chaos. Maybe beauty is chaos."[21] *Playboy* magazine asked him about long hair and he said, "If you figure it out, you realize that all of

25

one's hair surrounds and lays on the brain inside your head. Mathematically speaking, the more of it you can get out of your head, the better. People who want free minds sometimes overlook the fact that you have to have an uncluttered brain. Obviously, if you get your hair on the outside of your head, your brain will be a little more freer."[22]

By the time I got to Indiana, after about a hundred straight hours with the cowboys and angels and dwarves and midgets and Eskimos, I actually felt completely and totally like I loved Bob Dylan. Me and five hundred thousand other people, I know, and I was behind the times, but it wasn't just some dumb little thing. Listening to Bob Dylan was like having all the hilarity and absurdity and ambivalence and beauty of life distilled into music. It felt like everything about me—my senses, brain, heart—opened up in some sort of passionate, intense, beautiful, expansive way. I felt some sort of urgency, about what I'm not sure, but I could hardly sit still. It was like fire.

But actually, I don't love Bob Dylan. I mean, how could I use that word when I don't have any genuine contact with a real live living other? I don't really know him. I just know his magnificence and his brilliance. I am attracted to his beauty, but I've never felt his skin. I have no idea what he smells like. He's not alive to me. Not really. And he doesn't know me. I actually don't have a relationship with Bob Dylan. Whatever sort of thing I have, it's not horrible and depraved, but it's more like idolatry than like love. And idolatry and love are really different.

There is no such thing as love outside of relationship. Karl Barth talks about love as what is revealed to us by "God seeking and creating fellowship with us." *Fellowship* may seem like an off-putting word, but it's God's desire to be with us, related to us. Love is God creating relationship, communion.

And that relationship, love, includes a lot, maybe everything that is. Barth says, "There is death and hell," whatever that means, "in the scope of this relationship."[23] And loving your neighbor, he says, is not so much helping them out as being pressed up against them in your fellow humanity. And that involves a lot. "Mortal headaches," he says, their impotence and misery and futility exposing your impotence and misery and futility.[24] Father Zossima says, "Love in action is a harsh and dreadful thing compared with love in dreams."[25] Love is almost like reverse idolatry.

Love isn't some discrete thing or feeling that you have or don't have. There's not a thing-y quality to it. It's not at all static. I'm not even sure if it's simply something you do or you don't do. It's more like, are you involved with an other or are you not?—with all the tons of things being involved means. I don't think love is one sort of feeling you have, or even one sort of action. It's like communion. It's being all tangled up, in a mess even, more than maintaining a stable position toward someone. Love is not like unconditional positive regard. Who could ever live with someone and have that? The people I regard most, I regard in innumerable ways, not all of them nice and pretty.

I mean, I sort of hate to say this, but I think I might feel more consistently positive about Bob Dylan than I do about my kids. This is what it's like for me to be alive with my children: I wake up in the morning and they are gorgeous to me instantly and I feel enormous things that I can't even explain, and we get through breakfast and they are delightful, and then Olivia accidentally spits toothpaste at Miles and there's five minutes left before they have to get picked up for school, and Miles spits toothpaste back and they are behaving like mean and crazy animals and I feel heat and intense screaminess, and they seem to feel the same to me and it's

27

intense dislike all around for a while. They get out the door finally, and I do the dishes. When they get home, I'm happy to see them—and every day we do the same sorts of things over and over again. Beauty. Anger. Fighting. Judging, even judging. Communicating. Not communicating.

Love is living (which is outrageous and inexplicable and not very coherent or simple) in relationship (which is often incredibly wild and beautiful and scary and sad and occasionally strangely mundane) to a living other who is always other, not far off and distant but definitely other than you, uncontrollable and incomprehensible, but revealing. Love may be more disturbing than stabilizing, more like intimacy than admiration, more like struggle than reverence.

Worshiping an idol is far simpler and less chaotic and more consistently pleasant than tangling with an uncontrollable other. It is no wonder at all that we are obsessive idol makers. Idolatry makes the mundane sacred. It's something that can give you a sense of equanimity and make you feel good, instead of something that wracks your gut and involves all your heart and all your soul and all your mind, which, c'mon, just has to involve a lot of craziness and darkness and blindness and anger and, I guess, just about everything we are—animal meanness, beautiful sweetness, sickness and blood and unbelievable gorgeousness. But it's a lot. Jeez.

It's surprising that the Bible talks so much about what we have with God as love. From a lot of what you hear, you might expect God to be above all that. Perfectly holy, beyond such sordid and ignoble goings-on, removed from this messy tangle, and untouchable. But to say that God is wholly Other doesn't mean that God is unrelated, far away. Ungraspable, uncategorizable, yes, but not untouchable. That God is Other doesn't mean that God resides far away in a castle in the sky wearing white gloves, peering down his nose at us from his faraway perch. "Clearly [God] 'is' in a very different sense from the way the world or human beings 'exist,' " says James Alison.[26] "Part of the genius of monotheistic Judaism [is] the realization that 'one God' is much more like 'no god at all' than like 'one of the gods.' "[27] God is very other, much more other than any other others. But as Barth says, that otherness very much involves God's being related to us. That the other cannot be comprehended or apprehended or made available to us when and where and how we demand does not mean the other cannot be close. In fact, Marion writes:

> Between God and man, incommensurability alone makes intimacy possible, . . . duality alone allows recognition, communion progresses within the separation wherein gazes are exchanged. Distance: only he can become my neighbor who remains forever outside of me and my doubles. Only he can stand with me who stands before me. . . . Distance buttresses the one against the other until they bless one another.[28]

Reading the Bible, you get the impression that faith in God, relationship with God, is more an intimate sort of tangling with the uncontrollable, even unnamable Yahweh than a neat solution or a removed worship. Jacob wrestles, Abraham haggles, the Israelites resist, the prophets wail and beat their chests.

To believe in a God who actually lives and is actually in relationship to us is much weirder than believing in an ideology. More uncomfortable, perhaps even slightly absurd. So I think a lot of times the church makes loving God seem more like the coherent simplicity of worshiping an idol, something that can be neatly prescribed. Like it has to do with a sacred place where you light candles, or it has to do with getting our lives in order, or it's somehow just more like the Bob Dylan thing, a sort of removed admiration, than it is like being all tangled up with a living other.

It might be in part because the tangle seems like a lot and idolatry is more appealing, and it might be in part because it doesn't feel like a real relationship with God is possible. As if the only option we have with God is a sort of removed worship, since we don't smell God or fight with God. I've never felt God's skin. I haven't seen God wake up in the morning and spit toothpaste. I think it might actually seem like we can't relate to God as an Other, we can only relate to god as an idol, because how on earth do I really, really tangle with an unseen God? I feel like I want to, like bring it on, man. Give me something to tangle with, and I'll tangle, but I need a little more sensory input. I don't want to make an idol to grasp, but I'd like to feel *something* in my hands. If there were just something I could actually grab by the sleeve, or throw in the dirt, or kiss, then I wouldn't need my idols.

I don't think it always seems like we have an actual, real, live, full relationship with God. But the witness of the Bible, the witness of the church, is fairly adamant that we do. We live because God breathes God's breath into our nostrils. We are created, sustained, and redeemed by that breath. We are actually in relationship with God more profoundly than we are in relationship with anything or anyone else. It's just not graspable. It's not comprehensible. I can't get ahold of it, not because it isn't concrete or real or sensory, but because it isn't graspable. I can't comprehend it, not because God is not with us, but because God is with us so thoroughly. I can't quite see it clearly, not because it's not all around me all the time, but because I can't fix it in my gaze. We can't grasp it, not because it's not there, but because God is the most profoundly alive, unfixable thing there is. A presence so enormous, so permeating, so thorough, that it's mistaken for absence.

Marion says, "The unthinkable enters into the field of our thought only by rendering itself unthinkable there by excess."[29] We cannot comprehend God's presence, not because it is somehow lacking, but because of its surplus, "which neither concept, signification, nor intention can foresee, organize or contain."[30] We're tangling with the Other nonstop all the time. It's what is all along creating, sustaining, and redeeming us. We don't live or breathe or walk or talk outside of our relationship with God. We are so tangled in it, so thoroughly and completely in it, we can't comprehend it. It comprehends us. This is all outrageous and odd and pretty much the central point of Christianity. We live by the grace of God.

We seem to have idolatry in our DNA. But maybe at the deepest level we are not idolaters; we are people who need relationship. We are created in and for communion. We need love and relationship to breathe. But somehow, allowing ourselves to enter into communion, or to be who we really are, is more difficult or scary or unsettling than giving our lives to our belief systems, cultural codes, ideologies—our idols that aren't alive. And our idolatry freezes and fixes and suffocates and knots and nooses and guts and stuffs and kills. The Bible witnesses, however, to a God who keeps calling us into life; keeps creating life, life, and more life, bringing life from barren wombs and shoots out of dead stumps; actually resurrecting. This may seem like a bit much, but the Bible presses on and on: God is a God of life. James Alison talks about the sort of power that characterizes God as that of "being completely and entirely alive, living without any reference to death. There is no death in God. God has nothing to do with death." Alison refers to God as "God, the entirely death-less."[31] And it seems like God wants us to come along with him or her in this deathlessness. What could God be thinking, calling us into everlasting life? It might seem more responsible of God to call us to a simple coherent system, to organize a schedule of burnt offerings, to give us a way to redeem ourselves by following orders or rules or whatever, instead of redeeming us in relationship through love. It's frustrating. It's gorgeous. No wonder we are relentless idol makers, but God calls us to life.

The Bible witnesses to the entirely deathless one, to the living Word. It calls us to relationship with the Other. The Bible points us to this tangle. But often instead of allowing it to point us there, we use it somehow to get out of the tangle. It's both unbelievable and not at all surprising that we do this—we're dying for certainty and stability and a firm place to stand. But believing that's what we have in the Bible, in the Word of God, we mistake the summons of the living God for a rock, and our relationship to scripture becomes more like idolatry than a living response to a living being.

2

Ancient Riddles

The Bible is a very weird book. Sometimes I can hardly believe what is in it. It is not all nice and helpful and instructive wisdom. It is full of uncivilized stories, strange characters, and embarrassing outbursts. Like the story in 2 Kings 2:23–24 where some little boys tease Elisha, the prophet, "Go up, you baldhead!" and Elisha curses them. Immediately two bears come out of the woods and eat the little boys up. Or there's the part in Numbers 5, where it says if "jealousy comes upon" a man and he is afraid (maybe paranoid) that his wife has been with another man, he can go to the priest, who will cook up some little magic potion for her to drink, "the water of bitterness." If she has been with another man, the potion will cause her horrible pain and her body will swell up, "and her thigh shall fall away," whatever gruesome thing that means. If she hasn't been sleeping with any other men, the potion won't cause her horrible pain, and she'll be "free" to get pregnant. That's a little bit of an embarrassing thing to have in your Holy Book. Or how weird that the Good News of Jesus Christ in Mark ends with everyone trembling and fleeing and being afraid? Or that place in Corinthians where it says, "Women should keep silence in the churches. For they are not permitted to speak"?

It seems like at many of the most critical moments in the book (creation, the giving of the law at Sinai, the Gospels) there are at least two versions and they never quite mesh. In the Old Testament the versions are so wound around each other that the stories sometimes don't end up making much sense. The narratives are garbled because of it, and proceeding through them in a clear, linear way is often not really an option. The Bible often says one thing in one place and a completely different thing in another place. And it doesn't even have the sense to try and hide all this weirdness and all these discrepancies. They have not been smoothed over. They remain staring up at you, blatantly, brashly, from the page. Often truly baffling and incoherent. Frederick Buechner says,

> One way to describe the Bible, written by many different men over a period of three thousand years and more, would be to say that it is a disorderly collection of sixty-odd books which are often tedious, barbaric, obscure, and teem with contradictions and inconsistencies. It is a swarming compost of a book, an Irish stew of poetry and propaganda, law and legalism, myth and murk, history and hysteria.[1]

We may want our scripture to fix things for us. We may want a map to help us navigate the outrageousness of being alive. We may want clear-cut morality, a voice ringing out above all others to finally settle things for us, but it's just not what you find in these texts. William Placher says, "The Bible is not a single master narrative that represses all other voices but a complex text in which many sometime conflicting voices can be heard."[2] He writes,

> The attempt to read it as a true set of propositions keeps running up against so many puzzles that it seems that either this text does not make any sense at all or else such approaches are going about reading it the wrong way. . . . Some of the puzzles strike home so immediately that, as Wittgenstein remarked in a very different connection, for a mistake, this seems too big.[3]

Placher suggests that "perhaps their very diversity and ambiguity represents part of the meaning of the two texts."[4] James Alison says that this is what the scripture of people undergoing revelation of the living God by the living God looks like.[5] Not linear history, not science, nothing like a formula, but rather more of a struggle. The Bible isn't really at all good at being an instructional manual. It's good at leading us into a tangle of wild poetry, heartbreaking stories, contradictions, twists and turns, the concrete struggles of a vast array of unruly, disparate humans being sought after by God. It's what the scripture of humans living not with a fixed point, a master ideology, an answer, a cultural code, but with a radically alive Other looks like. The Bible isn't a cage that contains God, making God available to take out or hang in our living room, it's a witness to the fecund, ungraspable Other (and our relationship to that Other).

If, however, what we're looking for is a map or a manual, the Bible has some qualities that seem to allow us to regard it as such. We can actually grasp the Bible. It's a book. We can hold it in our hands. We can pull it off the shelf, open it when we want, set it in our laps or on the breakfast table. We can pack it in a suitcase or lock it in a glove compartment. It doesn't whip around the room at will or smash us on the head. It actually seems fairly inert, like something stable we can keep a firm grip on. We can memorize it. It certainly has the look of a manual more than a relationship. You can open the cover and turn the pages and everything's numbered and it's in columns. It appears to be fairly neatly arranged in a manner that one can easily consult. I remember a copy I had of *The Living Bible*. It had questions in the front. Big ones and little ones, things like, What is life? and Is foreplay before marriage permissible? And then it gave you the numbers so you could look up the answers. I remember that this felt comforting. I think I used it a lot.

It's tempting to believe that all the answers are contained between the covers of this book, that it gives us straightforward divine direction. Imagine having that delivered into our hands. Living in relationship to an utterly gratuitous God we can't control can be the most gorgeous and transforming thing ever possible, but it can be very uncomfortable, a little like being undone, like having everything you're used to relying on taken out from under you, "being suspended," depending on an Other, being reborn. Idols appear to make the divine accessible. The Bible seems to slip so easily into that role. But God isn't in a book and the Bible doesn't do away with faith, that (enigmatic and potentially foolish-seeming) reliance on the Other coming toward us to transform us. The Bible is a witness to that Other.

The rock and the sword

Rock and *sword* were metaphors we used for the Bible in the church I grew up in. It's interesting: something hard and something violent. The hard was supposed to be comforting. Not quite in the way of a mother's arms, but in the way standing on a solid rock is comforting. And the sword was also comforting: not loving words whispered in your ear, not your mother's scent, but what you could use to defeat Tiamat the Sea Monster. I remember my youth pastor grasping the Bible in his hand and raising it into the air, making a triumphant sort of sound. Pastor Ben knew what we were going to face out in the world, temptations like demons slithering up next to us, enticing us with promises of pleasure. But we could rejoice because God had given us his Word, and as long as we kept it near, we could defeat whatever might be lapping at our ankles. We had our swords to defeat the chaos. Though our fellow adolescents might languish in the realms of foreplay and cigarettes, we would be protected by the Word. I think this was partly why we were supposed to carry our Bibles to school and basketball games, into coffee shops and Pizza Hut. In fact, it was better if we were never without it (slash, slash, kill, kill the slinking murky pleasure).

Sword drills were a prominent feature of youth group. Pastor Ben would yell, "Swords at the ready: Joel 2:7," or "James 4:7," generally some minor prophet or short letter that was hard to find. And we would all draw our swords, trying to be the first to find the bit of instruction or encouragement or warning that would help arm us for the fight. The winner would call out, "Joel 2:7: Like warriors they charge, like soldiers they scale the wall. They march each on his way, they do not swerve from their paths." And we would all put our swords back in the sheaths hanging from our belts, feeling armed and roused and ready for the next fight. There was something very kind and empathetic and loving about Pastor Ben and his hopes for us. He wanted to assure us, promise us, that we could stand firm on the rock and never stumble, that our sword would be sharp enough to protect us from anything. But it didn't really turn out to be true. The Bible didn't protect us from cigarettes or hormones or the awkwardness of being a thirteen-year-old human. It never even came close to answering all my questions.

Though I learned about the rock and the sword from the youth group of a fairly small and isolated and hyper-exclusive brand of Baptists, a surprisingly similar attitude toward the text seems to permeate Christian culture. The Bible is something we use in duels, or to plant our feet on. Fundamentalists seem prone to pelting people with non-negotiable hard little rocks. Verses are quoted like stones, hurled at people living the difficulties of life. But people incensed by the Religious Right often have their quotes to hurl back, verses from Micah or the Sermon on the Mount, bits of wisdom or morsels of good and radical ethics. People who don't care for religion much at all will sometimes still argue, "Doesn't the Bible say this? How can those Christians act that way when the Bible says this." I do it myself quite often. It's as if the truth of scripture is some static and fixed thing you can pull out or seize on, something settled that tells you how to behave, more than some sort of dense and lively, strange and astounding witness to our relationship with God, a very different sort of truth. I guess it's often how we use all kinds of texts—abstracting from them, using them, instead of entering them—though we seem to do it especially with scripture.

Barth says, "The question, what is within the Bible? has a mortifying way of converting itself into the opposing question, Well, what are you looking for, and who are you, pray, who make bold to look?"[6] People have a tendency to find in the Bible what they seek. And you can abstract some gorgeous pearls and juicy peaches. You can pull out some of the most beautiful poetry and pithy wisdom and radical ideas about loving the neighbor and serving the poor. You can also abstract terrible messages from it, though I guess what you think is terrible depends on where you're standing. But there's no question that this way of using scripture has contributed to oppression and repression and exclusion and violence and the destruction of the environment. Daily. Right now. All over the place, women and gay people and US citizens and Muslims and Jews, salmon and psyches and bodies, repressed, oppressed, killed by the sword of scripture.

To treat scripture as if it somehow contains the truth of God rather than something that witnesses to what is ever outside of its own conceptual horizons, and then bowing down before it or giving your life to it or believing in it, is to make it an idol. It may be understandable, but it's dangerous. Swords and rocks slash and bruise and kill. Making the Bible an idol gets people trying to conform their lives to words, measuring themselves against "it," not thou, not the other, but "it," and gets people measuring other people's lives according to "it" too. It's dangerous when people who don't have all the absolute answers at their fingertips think they do. It's dangerous when people believe they have access to the divine, to absolute answers, merely by opening the cover of a book. Instead of somehow inducting us into relationship with the living God, the Bible as an idol helps to uphold our ideologies, what we already know and think and believe (and provides justification for slashing and smashing what opposes that).

Ephesians 6:17 says, "The sword of the spirit . . . is the word of God." The Bible also says tongues and teeth are swords (Psalms 64:3; Proverbs 30:14). Hebrews 4:12–13 says, "The word of God living and active, sharper than any two-edged sword, piercing to the division of soul and spirit, of joints and marrow. . . . no creature is hidden, but all are open and laid bare." *Sword* may be a great metaphor for the Word of God in some ways, but here it doesn't sound like something we can carry in our sheath or tuck in our belt and use on other people. What is it like to be naked and exposed, to have your joints divided from your marrow? It sounds a lot different from being in possession of a clear message, from being armed and protected.

There is a lot of rock metaphor in the Bible. God is a rock like none other, a fortress, a stronghold. But the Word of God to Hosea seems nothing like a rock. It careens through his being. He performs the Word by marrying a harlot and having children with her and having his heart broken (Hosea 1–2). The Word of God comes to Jeremiah and he "speaks" it by wrapping a waistcloth around his loins, and then later tearing it off and stuffing it in the cleft of a rock where it rots (Jeremiah 13). In John the Word becomes flesh and dwells among us (John 1:14). The Word in the Bible comes in a lot of ways, but hardly ever as a nice clean piece of information, a simple answer. It is hardly ever like an object from which you can abstract truth by regarding it dispassionately, in a detached and theoretical way, like you might regard science or a mathematical formula.

People obviously can use the Bible in all sorts of ways; as confirmation of their particular cultural preferences, as a manual to guide their behavior, as wallpaper or fuel for a fire, but believing that the Word of God is something one can actually hold in their hand or wield at will is idolatry. It is different from faith that the Word of God is the living address of the living God. To have faith in the living address of the living God, admittedly, seems weirder than simply adhering to what we find edifying in scripture. Believing it's scripture because of its beauty and wisdom, or because

40

it gives us a path to righteousness, seems less absurd than believing it's scripture because it witnesses to the radically alive, loving Other. Yet part of the outrageousness of Christianity is its claim that the words lying static on the page may somehow, oddly, live.

More an octopus than a rock

It's always interesting when a word means something and also its opposite, like *bad*. Or I've heard the jazz guys say "That's sick" when you feel like you're about to die because of how the saxophone player just made everything you ever loved and suffered come out of his horn as music. But I'm thinking now of the word *inspire*. The dictionary says it means to rouse latent energies, to inhale, to breathe into, to animate, to make alive. When we talk about our scripture being inspired, however, we often seem to think it means something more along the lines of it being fixed. Not made alive, but set in stone. As if inspired by God means God told people a long time ago to write down certain things and they did. And those things are inerrant, absolute, fixed, and settled. As if God's inspiration stiffens the Word rather than loosing it, objectifies it rather than breathing life into it. Because the words are inspired, we should put them under glass in a museum, worship them more than interact with them, guard them somehow, or appreciate their finality more than take them out to play.

It's been a struggle throughout the history of the church to understand what it means to have an authoritative text— what to do with it, how to understand it. The church has often recognized the need to guard against bibliolatry, and the way it has often done this is to appeal to the Spirit of God. Donald Bloesch states clearly in his *Essentials of Evangelical*

Theology that God's Word is "not the Bible in and by itself but the correlation of Scripture and Spirit."[7] Luther says that unless the Spirit opens scripture, it is not really understood. Barth says that the texts, the words on the page, aren't the Word of God, the revelation, but the witness to the revelation.[8] The Word of God is not in the text, it's what happens in the struggle. The words aren't the Word unless the living God animates these words, makes them alive somehow, breathes into them so they are rousing and carousing, not black and white on a page. This is admittedly a weird thing to believe, but it is clearly a part of the outrageousness of faith. It may be odder than believing in a clearly delineated ethical system, but it is very much a part of the tradition.

Maybe we need to work on our metaphors for scripture a little. Try something other than *rock* and *sword*. Barth refers to the biblical world as "a moving, living organ."[9] Bloesch says it "is not fettered. It leaps and runs."[10] Psalm 119 speaks of the ". . . ordinances," which are ". . . sweet to my taste, sweeter than honey to my mouth." Mouth and tongues and lips and honey, living and leaping and running. I'm not sure how to work that into a coherent metaphor, but I like the direction.

Robert Alter suggests that it was actually an innovative goal of the ancient Hebrew writers

> to produce a certain indeterminacy of meaning, especially in regard to motive, moral character, and psychology. . . . Meaning, perhaps for the first time in narrative literature, was conceived as a process, requiring continual revision— both in the ordinary sense and in the etymological sense of seeing-again—continual suspension of judgment, weighing of multiple possibilities, brooding over gaps in the information provided.[11]

Instead of tying something down, the text begs you to get involved—requires it, really.

Alison says that when we read the text we often presume it is something that is stagnant and fixed, but for the Hebrew writers this was never the case. The Word was something that came alive by being read, performed. There is not something prior to our interaction with the text. Our relationship to it involves reading and language, speaking and hearing—this is not like standing on a rock. The "it" is really so un-"it"-y, so open to interpretation. It is not hard and fast. Immutability doesn't seem to be the nature of texts, of words. Words remain open and vulnerable no matter how we try to control them, no matter what boundaries we construct. They can mean something and its opposite. Try though we may, we can't control the wayward tendencies of language. This doesn't seem bad and scary. It seems relational, polyphonic, messy, living. Stability is not a word that describes the text very well. The Word is not facts or something on a page we can uncover.

Maybe it's more like an octopus than a rock, something more wriggly, something you can hardly keep track of, but it draws you in. And messes with you a little. It's not a thing that is laid out flat on a page; it's more of a creature that interacts with you to help you undergo something, dismantle something, usher you into relationship.

Reading the Bible doesn't sort everything out and set everything straight. It's more like being drawn into another world where lines break down and separations cease and you lose your sense of righteousness, of being a victim to everyone else's wrong, and your heart is broken open, your joints separated from your marrow. The Word of God isn't a series of flat narratives with clear points; it's a wild unmanageable, "moving, living organ."

Octopus obviously isn't a great metaphor. Octopuses seem menacing and slimy and maybe nothing like anything we'd ever want to tangle with, but living in relationship to the living God is different from defeating the sea monster to create order. It may sometimes even be like living with it writhing in and all around you and others. The Bible doesn't lay out a religion that defeats chaos once and for all; it points to a relationship that includes it.

Perhaps when the scripture is in any meaningful sense the Word of God, it is something you encounter but never possess. You can carry the Bible to basketball games, Pizza Hut, the drugstore, and the bathroom. You can read it every day and learn what you want to learn and extract hard rocks or peaches. Or perhaps you can approach it in a way that requires continual revision, seeing again, suspension of judgment, weighing of multiple possibilities, brooding over the gaps.

Christian orthodoxy has always had at its center the belief that what God wants is relationship, but somehow we've used the Bible to keep that at bay. As if we don't tangle, we possess. As if we aren't struggling with an Other, but relying on rock-hard certainties. The way the church often handles the text actually uninspires it, takes away its life. In search of answers, stability, certainty, clarity, and comprehension, we get out the nails and the lassos to fix it or capture it, and we end up choking the life from it. We may be dying for something to wield in the face of life's unruliness, but the Bible doesn't seem like a way to get a handle on things. Reading it closely, honestly, quizzically, doesn't actually set us straight as much as it rattles us, undoes us, sets us loose so that we might fall into the lap of God.

Unfixing

Though I grew up memorizing verses, among people who could not have stressed more emphatically the import of the Bible to my life (and afterlife, and pretty much every move or decision I made), the first time I honestly found the Bible interesting was when I studied it with John Linton. John taught a semester-long program for the Christian College Consortium at the Oregon Extension, an old logging camp in the mountains that had been converted to a school. Linton always wore a hat, usually a black ski cap, I think maybe in lieu of combing his hair. He came to class with a cup of coffee and morning stubble. I had a roommate who complained about his foul language. Though John had earned his doctorate in Hebrew and Semitic studies, he seemed to have read everything in biblical criticism, theology, literary criticism, and psychoanalysis that had ever come out about a text in the Bible. He moved slowly and could pause, silent, in front of the class for remarkably long periods of time. His mission, I think, more like that of a Zen master than a museum guide, was to take our rock and, maybe not exactly throw it on the floor and smash it, but push it and pull it until it broke open. He tried to free us to actually interact with the Bible instead of treating it like an idol. He tried to get evangelical or fundamentalist kids who thought they loved the Bible to actually read it, instead of ventriloquize and memorize it. That was hard work.

He'd sit in front of the class slumped in his chair and read something strange from John or Jonah or Mark and look at us all intently, waiting for somebody to respond. Mostly we sat there like dead fish with blank eyes. Occasionally someone would make a comment that sounded like they'd just been reading *The New Interpreter's Bible* or remembered something from Sunday school. It was as if we were programmed to speak about the text only if we had the "right" answers, the standard answers, only if we already knew what it said. What John loved more than anything was when someone would get riled or agitated or when they'd shoot back the most out-there interpretation you could ever imagine. He'd say, "Now we're getting somewhere." I don't think it was because anyone was getting anything right, but because somebody actually moved, showed some evidence of life.

It seems like the church has often discouraged us from bringing the full force of our curiosity to bear on the text. Like somehow it wasn't quite permissible to ask all our questions, or doubt anything, or go "This is absurd" or "This makes me angry" or "What the hell?" If it sounded like the Bible was saying something that didn't quite fit with the official story, then we should maybe not bring it up, of if we did, we'd be set straight. I can understand why the church does this. I do it. If someone reads the Bible and hears that they are judged and going to hell, I think, well, they aren't reading it right. Occasionally I have thought that there are certain groups of people who shouldn't be allowed to read the Bible at all—in the wrong hands it can be dangerous. But the attitude that we have to guard it from mishandling has not exactly set a tone that encourages curiosity.

The church has also had a tendency to want to make the Bible simple. If we don't make it easy for people to understand, then they won't understand, and that will be bad. The church is very concerned about getting the message out. Of course it is. But sometimes that gets us trimming and domesticating, reducing the text to sound bites, formulas, nice little packages that can be more easily sold. It doesn't exactly make people want to wander through its dense and hoary depths. The Bible ends up coming across as flat and bland and trite and tedious and familiar.

My Grandma Blue prohibited us from saying we were bored, something we wanted to say often when we were visiting her in Russell, Iowa, which consisted of a water tower, a post office, a feed store, and four or five dogs. And flies. She said if we were bored, it said something more about us than about what was around us. What occasion could we possibly have to say anything was boring? Bored meant we weren't noticing. She was the wife of a typewriter salesman in a smaller-than-small town, and she knew this in her bones. There were rats in the barn and bees in the flowers and games to be played and puzzles to solve and weeds to pull. There may have been only 150 people, but still—150 people! If you were noticing, the possibility of boredom was impossible. I think there's something about the way the church has handled the text that makes monotony where there could be wonder, a remarkable opportunity for play. But our senses have been dulled and numbed, our curiosity has been curbed.

Noah gets drunk, maybe has sex with his son. Jael, the wife of Heber, takes a tent peg and a hammer and softly drives the peg into an enemy general's temple, till it goes down into the ground. The word *stability* appears in the Bible a total of six times; *suffer*, about three hundred. Trees clap their hands and asses talk, and what about Delilah and Samson and the Song of Solomon? You could hardly find any more passionate or sexier stuff: "Sustain me with raisins, refresh me with apples; for I am sick with love" (Song of Solomon 2:5). The characters are rough and beautiful and thoroughly human. The gaps in the text are everywhere. There are so many occasions for curiosity.

47

Linton tried to pull it all up and splay it all out in the open so we would feel something about it. Not what we thought we were supposed to feel, but whatever we actually felt—outrage, skepticism, suspicion, hilarity. Questioning everything in his class was an indication not of irreverence, but of the complexity of engagement.

A questioning curiosity is the antidote to boredom, and as a friend once pointed out to me, also of anxiety. He said you could try to dislodge anxiety by looking around, being open to observing what was outside your control, instead of focusing inward on your fear. Nurture curiosity, he told me, instead of feeding dread. I don't think he meant I should google non-Hodgkin's lymphoma or childhood brain tumors on the internet (which doesn't, in my experience, do much to relieve anxiety). He meant something more like contemplate the different shades of green in the grass or listen to the sound of someone's voice. Pay attention to what is outside yourself, or even inside yourself, that you've not been allowing to surface. The church seems to have a lot of anxiety about what would happen if we didn't keep things under control, anxiety about what would happen if people were set loose to interact in a more naked way with life, the text, the history of interpretation, free to be less constrained by prescriptions. I don't think this anxiety comes so much from faith in God as from fear of life. A fearless (or at least less fearful) curiosity and a more naked honesty might free us to engage in a more lively way with the text.

One of Linton's favorite things to say was, "You gotta get a little loosey-goosey with the text." He didn't want us to come to the text with such a well-conceived notion of what it means that we would only reproduce and recite the stereotypical discourse. He didn't want us to see it only through the dominant institution's or our own habitual and unexamined lenses. He wanted us to play a little more like Charles Mingus than like my six-year-old daughter who's just learning to read the notes. He didn't want us to be afraid to improvise, to think, to feel, to surmise.

Linton wasn't anxious about the process of interpretation, about whether or not we were getting it right, because for him the important thing wasn't about us getting something right. He was relaxed about what we did. It wasn't about finding the "correct" interpretation or the one true answer or how we could apply the text in a helpful, practical way to our lives, getting a grasp on it. It was more a sniffing out the scent of Yahweh, who, I think, Linton was pretty confident had us in her grasp.

Studying with Linton, I got the sense that revelation might be real. Not ancient stone tablets, not something you could uncover or know or memorize, but something that happens. Revelation wasn't like a rule you learned from the text: don't eat meat or be gay or yell at your parents, don't hoard your money or be anxious. Revelation was more what we might hear in the process of engagement. It might not give us facts to cling to, but it might unravel the paradigms that rule the world—the empire, the graceless tit for tat, survival of the fittest—or the paradigms that rule our minds. It might turn the world or our world upside down and inside out. It might help us break free from the world of gods, the world of our idols. Maybe what people really need is not simple answers but the complexity of relationship with the living God.

The rabbis

The church's habits of reading sometimes seem so guarded and domesticated that in order to break free from them we could stand a little outside help. There is beautiful and surprising Christian commentary, but lately I am eager to lap up anything I can find on the text from outside the protected fold—poststructuralist literary critics, a Mahayana Buddhist reading of Mark, a Lacanian psychoanalytical reading. These readers may not share my faith, and I may not share their conclusions, but they seem able to engage with the text in ways that shatter some of the unmoving appendages of the rock-hard idol. Perhaps we've just lived with the texts so long that it's difficult to come to them time and time again with new eyes, but perhaps our difficulty has something to do with how Western Christian culture has conceived of truth seeking, with our unconscious tendency to make the Bible an idol.

I know very little about the rabbinic methods of interpreting the texts, but my encounters with midrash have been mind blowing, or rock shattering, or something, at any rate, unfixing. It is like the first week of some super-intriguing class for me. I have learned just enough about the subject to know it would take years before I could speak intelligently about it, but I am so excited by what I've learned on my first day that I want to launch into revelries and rhapsodies about it with my roommate or in the cafeteria. It's like I've made a new friendship, me and midrash, though I actually barely know her, have barely shaken her hand, barely opened the first page. Still, I'm going to go ahead and launch (hopefully with respectful caution, but at least with this confession).

As a Christian used to Christian commentary, I am struck by how the rabbinic mode of reading seems to counter many of our idolatrizing tendencies. Susan Handelman in her book *The Slayers of Moses* discusses how the interpretive methods of Christianity were poised to go in a certain direction when it "severed its ties with Judaism, [and] became allied with Greek philosophy."[12] She argues that this split and new alliance have had a profound effect on the history of interpretive methods in the Western world, how the West relates to texts, how we believe meaning is conceived, "how we . . . understand understanding."[13] She contrasts rabbinic thought and the rabbinic mode of seeking truth to patterns that as Christians we are more familiar with.

In her introduction to her book on Exodus, Avivah Gottlieb Zornberg contrasts "the midrashic model for reading texts" with the Greek, which she quotes Isaiah Berlin as summarizing:

> The "Platonic ideal" in the history of philosophy . . . posits that all genuine questions must have one true answer and one only, all the rest being necessarily errors; in the second place, that there must be a dependable path towards the discovery of these truths; in the third place, that the true answers, when found, must necessarily be compatible with one another and form a single whole, for one truth cannot be incompatible with another.[14]

This seems to be the assumption that has often guided the church's pursuit of understanding. Truth or meaning will be coherent when found, stable, a solution to "the cosmic jigsaw puzzle."[15] Rabbinic modes of seeking truth are quite different, according to Zornberg.

Though I learned at the Bible Baptist Church in Kokomo, Indiana, that a biblical text always has one simple and coherent meaning that we may count on, that sort of thinking didn't actually originate with fundamentalist Christianity. The idea that truth is static and singular probably originated more from Plato than from Pastor Strohben, though Pastor Strohben and other fundamentalists have taken to it with great passion. It has been an assumption that has guided much of Christian exegesis across the spectrum, including the historical-critical method and social-science analysis and much of what has come down the Christian line. Growing up a fundamentalist, I was stunned when I finally encountered the historical-critical method at Yale Divinity School, thrilled at how it opened up the text in new ways. Now I am interested to learn how reading with a whole different set of assumptions might turn and scramble and open what we sometimes think we have a lock on.

I have this quote taped to the wall in front of my desk: "The sole criterion for an interpretation is its fecundity."[16] I like how it challenges the assumptions that I grew up with, and also what I learned at a comparatively liberal seminary. Harold Bloom says, "We need to read more strenuously and more audaciously, the more we realize that we cannot escape the predicament of misreading."[17] The proliferation happens regardless of what we intend, with preachers out there in a million different churches every Sunday, with people reading their Bibles in Iowa and Moscow, but it hasn't been exactly the way of Christian interpretation to intentionally propel us to fecundity. We seem to feel quite cautious of it, and for good reason. I know there were tons of rules that guided rabbinic interpretation. I don't know much about them or how exactly they were applied, but however it worked, they apparently allowed, even encouraged, a rich and wild fertility while still very seriously upholding and honoring and loving the Word.

Western Christian interpretation has often feared incoherence and multiplicity. Perhaps that fear has caused us to ignore some of the text's lush and equivocal, unruly and boisterous qualities. Perhaps it's caused us to fix it, stuff it, kill it, make it stone. The rabbinic modes of reading aren't constrained or determined by that same fear. Christian interpretation often assumes that if a text is obscure and ambiguous, it is because we have yet to solve the puzzle. For the rabbis, on the other hand, ambiguity was not a problem to be solved, but an occasion for "a multiple play of interpretation."[18] Far from fixing and taming and knotting and noosing, the rabbis appear to get "a little loosey-goosey" with the text.

Midrash, Zornberg says, is "a quest for God in our midst."[19] And that quest isn't much like looking for an answer, a simple and coherent stasis, a rock, a stable thing. It's more like encountering the Word of a God who speaks rather than statically exists.[20] Midrash is boldly looking and listening more than nailing down and fixing. It seems to reflect a little more of what it's like to be living beings in relationship to the living God than, say, the historical-critical method does.

The rabbis didn't pretend that they were not a part of the process, though objectivity has often been the stated goal of Christian interpretation. They didn't stand back from it with some sort of analytical detachment, with the goal of determining some objective meaning. They seemed to believe that you get to truth or to God more by relating, intimately, thoroughly, perhaps even incautiously, than by maintaining a stance of detachment. The plurality and multiplicity of readings were part and parcel of that process. Zornberg says, "The midrashic literature presents a heterogeneous, even—consciously and ambivalently—a heretical multiplicity of answers."[21] It is a different attitude from the one you get from most Sunday-school teachers.

Perhaps it is our anxiety and our seeming need to fend off chaos that has kept us clinging to the platonic ideal, needing to assume stability. But if truth is somehow living in a loving relationship with an utterly deathless God, then going after the truth with those assumptions may not be the greatest way to seek it. God is not the solution to a jigsaw puzzle.

"Rabbinic thinking presents us with a process, not a product," says Handelman. [22] It looks to me like an intimate, sensory, loving, and non-objectifying process. To be intimate with the Word, you burrow into its nooks and crannies. You eat it and taste it. You can't know it by being theoretical and detached. You don't suffice yourself with the surface; you seek to penetrate the surface. There may be meaning hidden in the most trivial and inconsequential detail. You don't pass over what at first seems familiar; instead "you turn it, and turn it," [23] and turn it again, looking for the hint of an intonation, a whiff of a scent, some crack that will let you inside. Stephen Moore says, "Victorian scruples regulate our reading habits. We need to rendezvous with the texts in the kitchen garden occasionally, away from the cloying niceties of the drawing room." [24] The rabbis seem much less constrained by "Victorian scruples."

For the rabbis, "Every vowel and letter is a meaningful sound, subject to inference and interpretation." [25] Rabbinic thought called for intense concentration on the words and their relations—even the physical shape of the letter and the punctuation. You can read the Bible in a way that you imagine is purely cognitive, or you can read in a more sensual way, noticing how the words feel when they cross your lips, how they sound when they reverberate in your ear. You can look at a letter and notice its physical presence, the curves, the spaces. Reading and listening are sensory experiences as well as cognitive. The rabbis don't seem as inclined to pass over the senses as were the Bible Baptists. The sound and the feel and the look of a word are important as well as what is signified. So they play with words and the sounds of words because it matters how things sound and how they feel in their mouths. This might have seemed "crude and barbaric" [26] to Greek philosophy, but it is very much the way of poetry. Moore quotes Jane Gallop as saying, "Once one starts attending to the odd truths revealed in the accidental material of language, one is led into a different kind of reading, no longer a sublimated relation to the spirit of the text, but an intercourse with its body." And says Moore, again referring to Gallop's words, "such intercourse would not be based upon the [male?] myth 'of the book's or the self's or the body's virginal wholeness.'"[27]

The Christian church has often had an antisensual bias (to put it mildly). Maybe in part because the body doesn't contribute that much to the notion that truth is static and eternal. Whatever our senses and drives are up to, it doesn't always seem to exactly fit with the project. When rational coherence and objective certainty and unchanging absolutes are god, the body doesn't play such an important part in the search for truth. For a faith that has God incarnate, God in body, at its center, this always seems a little unawake. The disaster this antisensual bias has wreaked in innumerable ways has been written about eloquently and often. It has caused many to dismiss, attack, and hate the church, and for good reason. This antisensual tendency has pretty thoroughly affected our interpretation of the text, how we read it, and what we believe is in it. We've often been convinced that the text itself encourages this tendency. The rabbinic way of reading doesn't seem to rest so much on the deeply implanted Greek dualism of body and spirit.

When Nietzsche describes the idolatry of the philosophers and theologians, talking about how they threaten the life of whatever they worship, he mocks them as blaming the senses for their inability to maintain a coherent and singular universalizing concept. They wonder what deceives them, and they "cry ecstatically, 'it is the senses! These senses which are so immoral in other ways, too.'" Anyone who believes in the senses, they say, has faith in lies. In their quest for truth they say, "Above all away with the body!"[28] Perhaps calling the senses back, reading more as embodied beings, could contribute to the unfixing.

I'm not sure exactly where I got the impression, but somewhere along the line I learned that midrash was somehow irresponsible interpretation. The rabbis made up stories that were tangential flights of fancy unwarranted by the text. But upon reading midrash, at least through the eyes of Zornberg, I am struck by how much these flights of fancy were like Christian preaching—a way to seek a living Word. It was legitimate. It was faithful interpretation not to leave the gaps be, but to fill them. Not with certainty, but with fascination. Seemingly unpropelled by the anxiety that often propels Western interpretation, the writers of midrash didn't fear the gaps or try to brush over them. The silences weren't locked vaults, but open caves. They were occasions for wonderment, for generating more narratives, ones that might be hidden in the cracks of the text. The midrashic narratives bring out what is not necessarily conveyed on the surface of the text but what is latent there. Zornberg says, "Without the black-on-white words of the scriptural narrative nothing can be generated, but without the evolving 'languages,' idioms of redemption, the foundational rapture recedes beyond recall." She says it is "the weakness, the gaps, the 'unthought known' . . . in the narrative that paradoxically invites the future to discover the primordial energy repressed in the text."[29] She says the midrash are stories that generate and reveal hidden unconscious layered narratives of redemption.

So they tell stories to fill in the gaps. Wild ones. About Og the Giant, the pursuer of ecstasy, condemned in the flood but clinging to the side of Noah's Ark. Noah pokes a hole in the side of the boat and feeds the giant to keep him alive.[30] The rabbis speculate about what exactly it was that Adam and Eve ate, or what Noah fed the animals, or what the fight between Cain and Abel was all about. Midrash doesn't consider this unimportant or silly or absurd. God speaks and pauses, and even the pauses are full of redemptive possibility.

There's something about the rabbinic methods of interpretation that reflects insistently that the Bible is not an idol—a stable thing to stand on, a rock. A page of the Talmud (a collection of Jewish law and rabbinic teaching) looks different from most Sunday-school curriculum. It doesn't hide the complexity and unruliness and layers of truth-seeking; it plasters them all over the page. There's the smallest portion of law, and then above it and below it and around the sides and in the margins, there's all sorts of commentary on it, commentary from different times and from different parts of the world. The arguments and revisions are made plain. It is never pretended that there is agreement. This isn't even a goal. Reading it is to engage in debate. "The interpretive process is collective."[31] "Hence the paradox," says Handelman, "that while the Torah represents absolute and ultimate truth, this truth is never simple and single, but is always subject to interpretations; and the interpretation, while also divine, is to a certain degree a provisional and relative *process*. Interpretation generates further interpretation and further scrutiny of different aspects, possibilities, and situations." The various readings "do not cancel each other out, thus generating further interpretation."[32] The goal is not a cosmic solution to the jigsaw puzzle: it is something much more like life, not stable, but dynamic and unruly.

I'm sure if I lived in the world of rabbinic interpretation, I would learn that it is as capable of idolatry as I am, as Christians are, as capitalists, communists, humans everywhere are all the time. But it seems like looking at the ancient rabbis might cheer us and free us a little, help us get over some of our anxiety about what will happen to our text if we don't put it under glass, if it isn't absolute in quite the way we've imagined it. That the text is open and vulnerable and unlike an idol does not mean that everything will crash in some sort of horrendous relativity.

I had a professor at Wheaton College, Dr. Joe McClatchey, who always started class by having us sing some verses from Lamentations: "The steadfast love of the Lord never ceases. It's new every morning, new every morning." It seems to me now like something that could have been vaguely subversive in the halls of an institution that stresses an absolute and never-changing authority.

The Bible doesn't supply us with a neat package of timeless wisdom and moral certitude. It witnesses to what it is like to be living beings in relationship to the living God, what it's like to encounter the Word of a God who speaks rather than statically exists, a God who continually creates life and resurrects it, who seems interested in growing shoots from stumps, not cutting them off, making possibility where there was impossibility, loving more than fixing. It's maybe more like a love that is new every morning than something you can carry around, stand on, or use to fight duels. The Word remains open and vulnerable, and that's nothing to be afraid of. Maybe the Word in all its crazy uncontrollableness can be let loose and trusted, not to do what the church necessarily expects or even wants, but in some way slightly unfathomable to us, to break, save, love, and redeem the world.

The belief that the Bible contains the absolute truth of God, set in stone, is something that has permeated popular evangelical culture. People who are not Christians seem to think that part of being a Christian is to believe that the text is coherent and that we would be disturbed to know it does not say the same thing throughout, that it contradicts itself, that it is garbled and weird. I wish we could all be out about that, that we could say yes, we know it's garbled and weird. We have a very strange text as our scripture. Isn't that wild? Doesn't that say something interesting about faith? Religion? Idolatry? They are fairly predictable and orderly, but faith? In the radically alive, relentlessly loving, having-nothing-to-do-with-death God? What a crazy, beautiful thing.

REVIVING THE DEAD

Marrow

3

In the Beginning

In the beginning God created.

Genesis 1:1

Thinking about the beginning can lead you to some bound-less places, in the same way as thinking about the end can. You can't really go there without mystery immediately moving in all around. Most days I try not to think about it all that much because it can be a little distracting to the tasks at hand: what was before this, what will be after this, to infinity and beyond. My children are different. They prefer not to be distracted by the tasks at hand. I am trying to get them to change into their pajamas; they are trying to get me to contemplate infinity.

"Mom, what was before dinosaurs?"

A question to which I don't know an exact answer, but I say, "Different sorts of animals. It's time to get to bed."

And so they say, "What was before those animals?"

I say, "I don't know, nature or something." I'm never that good at this.

And they say, "Well, what was before nature?"

And I say, "Maybe God."

And they say, "What was before God?"

And I say, "God was always there."

And they say, "Well, how did God get there?—and 'something' and 'maybe' aren't very good answers." And I honestly just want them to go to sleep so that I can lie on the couch and watch TV.

"Mom, what's past the sky?"

"Space."

"What's past space?"

"I don't know. Another galaxy. I can't possibly answer that question." But they keep asking and asking until I start getting a little freaked out about space and time, or on better days, bask in the depth of the unknown. My kids push me up against the limits of my mind just about as routinely as I make them brush their teeth.

The account of the beginning in Genesis 1 pushes too. But though the mystery clings to every word the writer lays down, he doesn't much discuss it. He's not grappling with the astrophysical dynamics of the origin of the universe. He's telling us about the beginning of a relationship, and we should probably think about it that way, listen to it that way—not like we listen to Science Friday or read a textbook, but more like how we might hear a love song. Genesis 1 is poetry. It's a love story. There's certainly always mystery in a love story—weaving in and out of what you know is always what you don't know—but it leads you to a different place than scientific inquiry, than the Big Bang and Neanderthals.

"In the beginning God created."

That's actually an abrupt start to the whole thing. In the very first line of the very first chapter of the very first book of the Bible, the involvement begins. Philosophy and theology often begin their discussions about God by discussing God as Godself, but the Bible doesn't. You almost wish it would; you'd practically expect it to give us a little something on the great autonomous being, a little information about who God is apart from us. You might expect a paragraph or two of God alone with no disruptions, God sitting serenely on some verandah on the cusp of creation sipping coffee contemplatively in perfect solitude. Perhaps at least a couple of lines about God alone with nobody, nothing making noise, no one complaining about what his sister is doing or asking for a drink. Instead, immediately God creates.

Great men rise to the top alone. Great warriors, the Jedi Knights, Harry Potter, and Spiderman cannot allow themselves to become attached. Attachment will compromise their heroics. The moment Anakin Skywalker becomes involved with Padme, his ability to be a salvific leader is jeopardized. Instead of wise and dispassionate nobility, there will soon be passion. Instead of pure and quiet strength, there will be jealousy, anger, raging desire. Involvement will somehow lead to weakness. The great, the strong must go up alone. Yet God comes down and creates, not God's masterpiece exactly, but the other whom God will doggedly pursue.

"To have a partner, while remaining in the mode of greatness, is an existential impossibility," says Avivah Zornberg.[1] To have an other with whom you must reckon, speak, struggle, feel, love, fight—it messes with you, distracts you, derails you from your path. In the beginning God created. That's the story in the Bible. God's first move could be seen as something that was bound to diminish God's greatness. God's not going to be autonomous and unaffected and dispassionate and alone. God immediately binds Godself to the earth, creates it, gives birth to an other to whom God will relate. It seems like a potentially reckless thing to do. Untold hazards open up. There will be no serene mornings sipping coffee in bed. Instead there will be someone constantly messing up the house, constantly interrupting your solitude, breaking your stuff, breaking your heart. Creating ushers in all sorts of possibility, and not all of it neat. We often hear the story in Genesis as if it's all about God ordering chaos. But if something like that is happening in the first four days, then by the fifth with the *swarms* of living creatures, and the great sea monster, and every living creature that *moves*, and with God saying to all that moving swarm, "Multiply," it sounds like it gets messy.

On the sixth day, the story says, God takes God's hands and puts them into the dirt and forms man out of the clay. Zornberg alerts us to the midrash by Rashi, "Everything else was created by an *act of speech*; only man was created *with the hands of God*."[2] God did not stand back and think humanity into being; God had God's hands all over the dirt, rolling it, spitting on it to wet it to mold the lips and form the toes. There are other places in scripture that speak as if God gave birth to the people from God's womb (Job 31:13–15, Isaiah 46:3–4). The image is not of a scientist cerebrally calculating the origins of humanity. We come from the hands, from the womb. God creates, engages in an activity that surely splatters mud on the wall or blood on the carpet. The relationship of the hands to the work, of the mother to the child in her womb, is a relationship that is the opposite of abstract and detached. It is a relationship of intimate involvement. In the beginning God engages in the muddy, or the bloody, the potentially heart-wrenching process of creation.

Genesis 1 isn't a poem in praise of some primordial condition of unitary being; it's a story of creation. It leads not to simplicity and nobility and stoicism, but to an inevitably complex experience. Just look at what follows the first chapter of the Bible. Just read the book. It's chaos, it's tragedy, it's comedy. It's not about heroes, great men who rise to the top alone. Creation seems to set off the possibility of so much passion, pain, betrayal; it surely goes a different direction from "control." Genesis 1 isn't about some wonderful primordial undifferentiated union, but creation for the sake, perhaps, of a more complex unity—for the sake of love.

In the very beginning of this story of God, what we hear is not something that should send our mind to rational calculations about dinosaurs and the Big Bang, it's more like something that might evoke a response, a response that we might have to a lover or a mother who says, "I love you" and means it. Means it in such a thick and foundational and enduring way that it is as unfathomable as infinity. Genesis 1 announces the deepest mystery, but it's not just mystery. It is the mystery that God so loved that God created: decided for us. God's greatness isn't in some rigid containment. God's greatness is love.

4

The Original Lie

Then the LORD God said, "It is not good that the man should be alone; I will make him a helper fit for him." So out of the ground the LORD God formed every beast of the field and every bird of the air, and brought them to the man to see what he would call them; and whatever the man called every living creature, that was its name. The man gave names to all cattle, and to the birds of the air, and to every beast of the field; but for the man there was not found a helper fit for him. So the LORD God caused a deep sleep to fall upon the man, and while he slept took one of his ribs and closed up its place with flesh; and the rib which the LORD God had taken from the man he made into a woman and brought her to the man. Then the man said, "This at last is bone of my bones and flesh of my flesh; she shall be called Woman, because she was taken out of Man." Therefore a man leaves his father and his mother and cleaves to his wife, and they become one flesh. And the man and his wife were both naked, and were not ashamed.

Now the serpent was more subtle than any other wild creature that the LORD God had made. He said to the woman, "Did God say, 'You shall not eat of any tree of the garden'?" And the woman said to the serpent, "We may eat of the fruit of the trees of the garden; but God said, 'You shall not eat of the fruit of the tree which is in the midst of the garden, neither shall you touch it, lest you die.'" But the serpent said to the woman, "You will not die. For God knows that when you eat of it your eyes will be opened, and you will be like God, knowing good and evil." So when the woman saw that the tree was good for food, and that it was a delight to the eyes, and that the tree was to be desired to make one wise, she took of its fruit and ate; and she also gave some to her husband, and he ate.

Genesis 2:18–3:6

Imagine being alone in a beautiful garden full of lilies and apples and nice animals, just tending to the fruit trees and naming all the creatures. It's not like you'd have to be sitting around unengaged all the time. You could ride elephants. You could learn to make fruit things—wine and pie. Maybe you could learn to make really good wine and sit on the banks of a meandering river and drink it, laying your head against the belly of a beautiful fuzzy tiger.

It wouldn't be like being alone in a world where you might feel left out. It would be impossible ever to feel left out. There would be no way to get in trouble. There would be nothing to make you feel bad. You could just be completely unselfconscious, naked even. There would be no shame, no one to judge anything about you, no one to blame you for anything. Alone, you would never have to worry about fat or wrinkles or if you were good enough. There would be no one to measure yourself against, no one to compete with. There'd be no struggle, just you and a loving God and animals to play with in the garden of pleasure.

It's not good for the human to be alone? I don't know. I mean, what is good? It seems like alone, I could potentially get the tranquil, nobility, holiness thing going a lot easier, and on the other side of the spectrum, I could access the totally unselfconscious abandon thing easier too. Extricated from all my entanglements with people, I might be a better, or happier, or freer person.

Of course that's completely silly, and it's not what I believe. I love love. I believe in relationship. But thinking about this story of what has so often been called original sin makes me question the ease with which I sometimes proclaim my allegiance to love. What really fires the synapses in my brain? What really motivates most of my activity?

God says it's not good to exist alone, and all of God's activity works toward communion. Creation, incarnation, redemption. Apparently to God—independent, solitary, transcendent, absolute glory—what we often think of as holiness is not good. Good is in relationship. Only. Really. There isn't even another possibility. It's so obvious, and it's also slightly mind-blowing.

Relationship is our life. We don't have life without it. We are conceived through relationship: the sperm and the egg. We are, as Alison says, "utterly dependent on other people bringing us into existence."[1] We wouldn't learn to walk or talk without relationship, without the other teaching us. The Buddha's practice of selflessness, says Robert Thurman, was based on "a complete technical, philosophical, and psychological" analysis, after which one must conclude that there is no such thing as an unrelated self. We are "caught in a distorted perception about the centrality of ourselves as fixed, independent, isolated entities apart from all others."[2] This is the delusion that humanity lives under. We can't know ourselves apart from relationship. There's no self apart from it to know. Alison says, "We are brought into being by what is other than us. Not just at birth, but over time. We are radically malleable and dependent. It's not bad. It's what being created means. It's what being a creature means."[3] It is outlandish that we would fight against our utter connectedness—break, avoid, deny this most basic reality in any way ever—but we constantly do.

Olivia, my six-year-old, sings a lot. She makes up songs constantly. Lately they've been a lot about love: "I believe in love. Love is beautiful. Love is the most important thing." I think she is delightful and I love her songs and I'm happy she's not singing about Barbies or hairdos, but I also have this feeling that these songs lately about love are a little canned, and I wonder if she's just reciting propaganda I've foisted upon her.

I talk about love a lot. I want my kids to believe in love. But I wonder, what does she think love is? Does she have any idea? And should she? And then I start thinking about it too much, and it starts to seem like love is something children shouldn't even speak of, like a knife that cuts you open and splays out every beautiful and every unpresentable thing. It's so full of discomfort and flaring hatred and us at our ugliest and weakest and us hating ourselves at our weakest and ugliest and hating the other for knowing us and knowing them. It's horrible. And beautiful. And at times full of the greatest disappointment a person could ever know. It's not all sweet, really, though it has its moments.

So, I thought, I should talk to Olivia about mercy more. Maybe I haven't been talking about mercy enough, and there's no love without it. So I tried, because I thought, there is so much pain in love, and I know she's going to suffer from that, and the hope is in the mercy. So I've been talking a lot about mercy, and she's been adding "mercy" to her songs lately. Now they are something like "I believe in love and mercy and love and mercy are beautiful." Which you think might seem good to me, but then I start thinking, wait—no, mercy? Suddenly it seems like it's practically X-rated, it includes so much. There's so much violence and brokenness and blood all around it. And I just think, gosh, maybe Olivia, my beautiful, sweet young daughter should sing about turtles or butterflies and not even remotely refer to what ends up being the story of how God undoes the violence at the heart of the human condition by being murdered and suffering and dying on the cross.

Of course, I've been thinking about the Fall, this passage in Genesis, so perhaps I'm being a little dark and dramatic. But it does somehow seem like relationship is fraught with so much pain. I believe in love. Who doesn't love love and believe in love? I believe that it is not good that we should be alone. But I also think there's something in me that questions, even denies, the very premise of my creation. And I think that somehow we do this from practically our first conscious moment. Somehow relationship becomes "problem" instead of salvation. Instead of the unselfconscious joy of being with an other, there is a great deal of tension involved in not being alone.

If we say we have no sin, if we say we love love, maybe we deceive ourselves. If we say we love the other, it's just the greedy corporate financiers, capitalist pigs, racists, or warmongers who don't love love—maybe we deceive ourselves. If we say we love love, it is just our roommate or wife or dad or husband or president who doesn't love love—maybe we deceive ourselves. I think this story in Genesis about original sin isn't so much about discovering whom or what we might blame, as it is about leading us to confession: the other is a bit of a problem for us.

One flick of the tail

The very first glimpse you get of relationship in this story isn't conflict or alienation; it's sort of an ecstatic eros. It's pretty sexy. The other faces the other and they say, "This one at last is bone of my bones and flesh of my flesh," and they are united and they are naked and they feel no shame. It seems nice and exciting. And then something happens. There's a lot of weight put on the something that happens as if it might explain everything—the tension, the brokenness— but I don't think it explains everything as much as it simply says it happened. Because how can you really explain a completely false thing that derives from nothing real? How can you explain something that has never been created, that has no real substance, nothing, no thing? Our life is in relationship. We are created in and for and by relationship. There is no life apart from it, and yet we resist it. This is the origin of idolatry.

Adam and Eve, the naked and unashamed couple, are having a conversation with a talking snake. The snake has been much maligned as the force of evil, Satan, though in the text he is "more subtle than any other wild creature that the LORD God had made." He is described as smart more than bad. Phyllis Trible says, "Certainly, he is the villain, but then the story itself is not about a villain." The focus here is on the humans, on whether they will be with God and for God, whether they will choose life or death. The snake "is a literary tool used to pose the issue of life and death, and not a character of equal stress. A villain in portrayal, he is a device in plot."[4] To imagine that with the snake we have a character to blame for the fall of humanity is to give the snake more "being" than he merits. Barth says, "The devil is that being which we can define only as independent non-being."[5]

God is not part of the conversation between Adam and Eve and the snake. They are not talking to God but about God. In fact, they are sitting around talking about God as if God's not there. God is objectified—not conversed with, but defined. God is not a subject in the relationship. And as often happens when people are doing that sort of thing, within about three sentences God starts to look like a completely different character. Instead of the lover, creator, life giver whose greatness is in relationship, in not being alone, God starts to look like some sort of icky, greedy, rivalrous, petty being all concerned about being separate. As if God is all about drawing a line to keep humanity away, to keep transcendence for Godself.

The snake makes it seem like when God says, "Don't eat from that tree," God is trying to forbid the really good thing, the most delicious thing, because God wants to keep it to Godself. As if there is more life to be had, but God says, "No way, you get this much and no more. This is mine and you can't have it." As if God is all about, "Hey, stay on your side of the line, man. Don't come any closer." As if God wants distance.

How in a paragraph does the snake spin a totally false god, and how can it be that that idol is so often precisely what we worship? The snake makes it seem like the absolute, the transcendent, the knowledge of good and evil—what is apart and above and static—is the good, more than what is with and among and living.

Maybe God is not actually a petty, greedy, rivalrous being all concerned with separation. Maybe with the whole tree thing, God was like, "Eat it all, man, all the life, it's yours—but that one tree is no good. Don't eat that." But the snake says, "If you eat that one, you'll be like god." What God? The god he just made up! The god that doesn't exist, a god who is absolute and self-sufficient and self-centered, "a supreme being rotating about himself."[6] With one flick of the tail, the snake redefines God and good and wise and desirable. If the humans here want to be like god, it is a completely false god, an idol. And worshiping that idol, wanting to become like that, sucks life and destroys relationship. It's death.

We're so mistaken if we think God doesn't want us to choose life, or forbids it somehow. It's death God doesn't want us to choose. The Fall isn't uncontrolled eros winning. The story isn't meant to keep us denying our humanity. It shows more that we make an essential break from humanity, step out of relationship for the knowledge of good and evil, make up a god, prefer to eat that, want that, worship that, than to be dependently co-arising.

It would be revelatory to recognize that somewhere we believe (or if not quite believe, then act in ways that suggest we believe) that it might be good to be alone—not just part of, but better than, bigger than, more important than. Not one with but removed from, set apart from, somehow transcending the masses. I think this story in Genesis might help us see that somewhere, consciously or unconsciously, we question the goodness of our relatedness all the time. Maybe this snake-spun false god is often what drives us, our paths in the world, our religious impulses, and our culture. We don't want to be a nation among nations. We want to be the biggest and strongest and freest nation. We don't want to recognize how we are connected to others, whether fundamentalists or the rural uneducated or rich elitists or the unenlightened or the oppressors, as if our ways have nothing to do with their ways. We think what will save us is extricating ourselves from the fray and judging it good or evil, more than recognizing ourselves as inextricably a part of it.

Alison says, "There is no properly theological approach to 'our first parents' that is not a discourse of love concerning the first people to need the sort of constructive forgiveness that we first discovered ourselves to need."[7] By keeping alive the doctrine of original sin, "the Church is not engaged in an accusation against humanity. What the Church is keeping alive is the possibility that even those who bear the tremendous burden of being 'right' may recognize their complicity with those who are not."[8] That is its creative potential.

5

A Midrash on the Tower of Babel

Now the whole earth had one language and few words. And as men migrated from the east, they found a plain in the land of Shinar and settled there. And they said to one another, "Come, let us make bricks, and burn them thoroughly." And they had brick for stone, and bitumen for mortar. Then they said, "Come, let us build ourselves a city, and a tower with its top in the heavens, and let us make a name for ourselves, lest we be scattered abroad upon the face of the whole earth." And the LORD came down to see the city and the tower, which the sons of men had built. And the LORD said, "Behold, they are one people, and they have all one language; and this is only the beginning of what they will do; and nothing that they propose to do will now be impossible for them. Come, let us go down, and there confuse their language, that they may not understand one another's speech." So the LORD scattered them abroad from there over the face of all the earth, and they left off building the city. Therefore its name was called Babel, because there the LORD confused the language of all the earth; and from there the LORD scattered them abroad over the face of all the earth.

Genesis 11:1–9

It's amazing how fast things move from the garden where God creates life and everything is fruitful and multiplying to a much more barren place. One minute everything is sprouting up and flowering, and the next there is tension and anxiety and rivalry and murder and violence, and God is seeing that "the wickedness of man was great in the earth, and that every imagination of the thoughts of his heart was only evil continually" (Genesis 6:5).

By only the eleventh chapter of the book of Genesis, the people are pretty far from the garden. They've arrived at a plain, a flat place where the men want to build themselves a city and a tower. They aren't naked anymore. They've shaved and cut their hair, and there's one language and few words. They live not amidst messy tangled growing stuff, all teeming with jillions of species, but on a plain. They don't want to watch things grow, pluck fruit from trees; they want to build something. No more lush, loamy fecundity. Now they say to each other, "Come, let's make bricks and burn them hard. Let's build ourselves a big, tall, hard tower."

They want to make a name for themselves. They don't want to be named. There was all this naming going on in the garden. Benson writes, "Marion says that the 'proper' name is 'given to me before I could choose it, know it or even hear it; it was given to me because in fact I was given.'. . . . My identity 'can be proclaimed only when called by the call of the other.'"[1] Naming is a big deal; it is a part of calling something into being. But the men on the plain don't want to be given a name; they want to make their own name. Trusting an other to call you into being, recognizing that you don't actually make yourself but are made by forces outside your control, is potentially unsettling.

It's also quintessentially un-American. Our culture thrives on a mythology that is all about being self-made. Our heroes rise up out of nothing by force of their own will. On the way to work last week, I turned on the CD player and got blasted by the soundtrack from *Pokémon: The Movie 2000*. Miles was apparently in the car before me. I let it go for a while out of curiosity, wondering what sort of messages Squirtle and Bulbasaur and Pikachu might have for my child. At first I thought it seemed pretty good. It seemed to encourage positive self-esteem, encourage kids to take on challenges. But then it went into this little verse about the power of one. How it all starts with believing and goes through the soul and changes the world, how each of us holds the key to the power of one. I got the definite feeling that the song was suggesting that you make whatever you will of yourself. You can do it. It's up to you. The power of one may be a lie, but it is a myth that America is made on. To think that you can't, don't, ever really make yourself is an offense to the American ethos.

God called the man "Adam." It might not have seemed like such a great name. *Adamah* is earth. Adam is the earthling, the one formed from dirt and the breath of God, not a self-made man at all. Perhaps that is just deeply disconcerting at some level, to be contingent, earthbound, malleable, and dependent. So the men say, "Let's build a tower in the sky and make a name for ourselves."

The story of the tower is a remarkable contrast to the story that precedes it, Noah's ark. God's redemption for the human predicament is to have Noah build an ark. The ark carves a curved space out of the water, a womblike enclosure where Noah will live very closely with family and with animals.

It's a place where he will learn their feeding schedules, how to care for them, how to live right up next to their smells and fur and feathers. He will have to deal intimately with their feces and their appetites. Noah becomes a feeder and a life sustainer. According to Zornberg, "The core of the ark experience is Noah's relation to the animals he brings with him."[2] It is "within the intimate but teeming space of the ark [that] Noah becomes, in the midrashic view, a new person."[3] She says, "To be totally present to the needs of the animal—this is the very meaning of the ark experience."[4] Noah learns the "capacity to nurture the needy, with the right food at the right moment. The knowing of need is the highest measure of [the] curious tender concern" that makes for redemption.[5]

What the men on the plain devise for their progress, their success, is not exactly a womblike enclosure that acknowledges need. They want a big, tall, hard tower. The ark and the tower go such different directions. The men on the plain didn't want to have their name in relation to the other; they wanted to make a name for themselves, and they wanted to make it big. *Big* is very often the unquestioned assumption for the direction of human enterprise. It is how men redeem themselves. The Noah's ark–type redemptive move, God's redemptive move, seems to go in a different direction. You could say, Noah learned to feed the hungry and that sounds pretty big, but what if redemption was a little like feeding the cat, your family, the next-door neighbor, or one guy you meet on the street? That seems little. Insignificant. And the men on the plain did not want to be that.

God tells Noah to bring into the ark "every living thing of all flesh, . . . two of every sort . . . , to keep them alive with you. . . . Of the birds according to their kinds, and of the animals according to their kinds, of every creeping thing of the ground according to its kind, two of every sort shall come in to you, to keep them alive. Also take with you every sort of food that is eaten" (Genesis 6:19–21). What a cacophony there must have been on the ark. Pigs snorting and cows mooing, birds singing and giraffes doing whatever it is that giraffes do, and every creeping thing creeping all over. What an insane diversity of sounds and smells and needs. In order for Noah to keep all of them alive, he had to learn how to respond to an enormous variety of hungers, to store up "every sort of food that is eaten."

One language and few words may seem barren in comparison, but it is a better situation for the tower project. It assures easier and more efficient communication, less cacophony, more clarity. So they took bitumen and mortar and bricks to construct their unshakable edifice. The people believed in what they were building. How could they not? It's what consumed them. If you weren't contributing to the building, what was the use? What else would you do? If you weren't making a name for yourself, what were you even doing? Maybe there were people who questioned the project, people who thought they didn't mind being named, thought they might like playing in the weeds, thought tents would be fine. Maybe occasionally there were even people who felt like hurling bombs at the place, but even they were consumed with the tower.

There's another story a little later on, in Exodus, where the people of God have become slaves and their task is to make bricks. And there are other places, still later on, where God tells the people that if they forget their covenant with God, they will end up serving gods of wood and stone, "the work of men's hands, that neither see, nor hear, nor eat, nor smell" (Deuteronomy 4:28).

It may have seemed preferable somehow to serve something that didn't see or hear or eat or smell, to make bricks and to serve the tower project. Perhaps seeing and hearing and eating and smelling didn't feel like very honorable tasks, really, or all that redeeming—like feeding voracious, smelly animals in the ark. Feeding and seeing and hearing an other was such a messy business, such a frustrating process, sometimes you could hardly call it a process at all. *Progress*, *success*, weren't the best words for it. You couldn't very easily make a name for yourself that way, but making the tower was clearly progress. So they said to each other, "Let's make bricks." Never mind that brickmaking later becomes the occupation of their slavery; they made a lot of them.

But then God comes down. God says, actually, let "us" go down, like God talking to Godself, not like wood or like stone, but like God in Godself speaking and hearing and moving and living. God comes down, which is pretty much the opposite direction the people were trying to go, and God looks at what they're doing and is interested in what they're doing and sees the way they're going and says, You know what? They're just going to keep going this way, building this building, even though in some ways, it's not working out all that well for them. The names they are making are fabrications. They may look all right, but there's all this underlying anxiety. The foundation of this tower is hard: brick-hard fear. Not trust, not love and grace and mercy. The foundation is "a futile exercise in the production of a fragile order."[6] So the Spirit of God blows through the building and confuses their language, tells their few words to be fertile and multiply, and though everyone's scattered, they are freed from serving the god of wood and stone, the work of their own hands. "They left off building the city."

At creation, God named the people God's own: *Beloved.*
God loved them into being. What if our only *real* significance
comes from being called into being by an other, and it's not
really little at all, it's huge, it's the hugest thing, it's all that
really matters? What if building the tower is really the thing
that is little and insignificant and vanity and futility, and our
only real task is to love our neighbor, but some inexplicable
anxiety, some lack of trust, makes us leave our place in love
to make a name for ourselves? And we end up serving gods
of wood and stone, the work of our own hands, gods that
don't see or hear or eat or smell.

So, the story goes, the city they built to make a name
for themselves is called Babel. That's Babylon, the place of
noncommunication. At one level, it's a fake story: this isn't
really how Babylon got its name. Etymologists know this.
But it's a story that reveals the futility of the empire's enterprise. The name that ends up being made is Babel, the place
of noncommunication, the tower of not-love.

The story is the strangest mixture of hopeful and hopeless.
We are really, really held in love and made for love, but then
we leave and leave and leave, and believe in our building,
and are so afraid and anxious, and seem so far from love,
trapped in our tower in Babylon. But then God keeps following us around and freeing us and calling us back.

In the book of Acts, we read that the Spirit comes down
at Pentecost, and when the Spirit comes through, everyone
begins to speak in different tongues. But though the speech is
all confused and the vocabulary unlimited—words you never
heard before—the people somehow miraculously understand
each other, and they see and hear and feed each other. And
that is the church. I think the Spirit blows all through the
tower all the time, and it isn't the work of our hands.

6

God's Mouth on Our Nostrils

The hand of the LORD was upon me, and he brought me out by the Spirit of the LORD, and set me down in the midst of the valley; it was full of bones. And he led me round among them; and behold, there were very many upon the valley; and lo, they were very dry. And he said to me, "Son of man, can these bones live?" And I answered, "O Lord GOD, thou knowest." Again he said to me, "Prophesy to these bones, and say to them, O dry bones, hear the word of the LORD. Thus says the Lord GOD to these bones: Behold, I will cause breath to enter you, and you shall live. And I will lay sinews upon you, and will cause flesh to come upon you, and cover you with skin, and put breath in you, and you shall live; and you shall know that I am the LORD."

So I prophesied as I was commanded; and as I prophesied, there was a noise, and behold, a rattling; and the bones came together, bone to its bone. And as I looked, there were sinews on them, and flesh had come upon them, and skin had covered them; but there was no breath in them. Then he said to me, "Prophesy to the breath, prophesy, son of man, and say to the breath, Thus says the Lord GOD: Come from the four winds, O breath, and breathe upon these slain, that they may live." So I prophesied as he commanded me, and the breath came into them, and they lived, and stood upon their feet, an exceedingly great host.

Then he said to me, "Son of man, these bones are the whole house of Israel. Behold, they say, 'Our bones are dried up, and our hope is lost; we are clean cut off.' Therefore prophesy, and say to them, Thus says the Lord GOD: Behold, I will open your graves, and raise you from your graves, O my people; and I will bring you home into the land of Israel. And you shall know that I am the LORD, when I open your graves, and raise you from your graves, O my people. And I will put my Spirit within you, and you shall live, and I will place you in your own land; then you shall know that I, the LORD, have spoken, and I have done it, says the LORD."

Ezekiel 37:1–14

It's a little hard to ask this question without feeling embarrassed. It seems like something a sixteen-year-old lying on her bed staring at the ceiling would contemplate, or a stoner. It seems cliché and hokey, but—what is life? I talk about it like it's everything, but what is it even? It's obviously physical, but I wouldn't say that a heartbeat is an adequate summation of what life is. Things are alive that don't have a heartbeat, and you can have a heartbeat and, I think, be less than alive. Whatever life is, it seems to cause us anxiety. We really want it and we're afraid it will pass us by, so we desperately grab and hoard it. Or else we're a little afraid of life and try to keep it in a cage, feed it dried dog food once in a while and pet it occasionally. It seems like both of these tendencies are somehow detrimental to the life of the world.

The dictionary doesn't even do a great job of defining life. It mostly defines it over against death, which seems right but is still a little evasive. Wikipedia says there is no universal agreement on the definition of life, "though the generally accepted biological manifestations are that life exhibits the following phenomena: organization, metabolism, growth, adaptation, response to stimuli, reproduction."[1] There are, however, obvious exceptions to these rules, like mules and ant workers who can't reproduce. And going with that definition might force us to include viruses, flames, and software programs. Some scientists maintain that life on this planet is based on the chemistry of carbon compounds and assert that this must be the case for all possible forms of life throughout the universe. But this position is referred to as carbon chauvinism, and that doesn't sound so great.

Emmanuel Levinas says, "Life is *love of life*, a relation with contents that are not my being but more dear than my being: thinking, eating, sleeping, reading, working, warming oneself in the sun. . . . The human being thrives on his needs."[2]

Maybe it's impossible to agree on what life is. It may be nearly as difficult to agree on what life is *for*. In America today, one might get the impression that real, full, satisfying life worth living requires an audience. There are websites that match people willing to do preposterous and humiliating acts with people willing to pay to watch them and film them. People covering themselves in molasses and birdseed and letting pigeons eat it off their body for $300, a guy willing to strip to his underwear on Wall Street for $700. A man ate dog shit in front of an audience for $400. As John Seabrook wonders in *Nobrow*, his book on popular culture, "Is this an outrage in taste, or is it something more, a fundamental misconception of what reality is—a mass delusion shared by an ever-greater number of people everywhere?"[3] What is life and how do we get it? Seabrook quotes the director of New York's Public Theater: "The whole concept of the journeyman artist has disappeared. You are not allowed to go on a journey. There is no journey. You're either extraordinarily brilliant or you're dead."[4]

Does our culture generate something that seems like life but is really more like death: a thousand colors of plastic, the commodification of every last thing, packaged pleasure and lifestyle, Ikea? Do our pursuits lead to life or to death? Maybe both, I don't know. I hardly know what I'm talking about. It seems like people can identify things that make them feel alive, but is feeling alive the same as life? I wonder if teenagers driving tanks in Iraq, listening to rock and roll about shooting and killing and kicking ass, feel pumped up with "life"? I kind of think so, but can you call it life if you feel alive while you are doing a death-generating thing? What is life and how do you get it?

A heap of dry bones

It is really hard to believe that we actually get our life from God, that life depends on God, that God is the breather of life and without the breath of God there would be no life. Maybe we can accept that in some metaphorical or spiritual sense God gives us life, but not really, not biological life, not like breathing and moving and eating and feeling and warming oneself in the sun. I can claim it up and down and back and forth for the sake of my argument, but it is not something that I honestly live in awareness of on most days, or even believe on a regular basis.

It is nevertheless what the Hebrew scripture and the New Testament and the church ask us over and over again to believe: God is life, the creator and source of life. The stories often go so far as to claim that as long as people knew their life depended on God, they were walking in life, and when they didn't, they were walking in death.[5] Whenever they attributed life to something other than God, believed in other things as the source of life, they were clamoring after idols, they were generating death. That could seem like a ridiculously sweeping condemnation of everything we do, or it could seem like someone desperately wanting to free us to live.

I don't know at what level we're really capable of believing that our life depends on Yahweh, but it is a fairly crucial part of the story. God is the breather, and without the divine breath we don't even breathe. Our life hangs on a breath we do not control. We become alive only in this encounter with God. And without the repetition of this breathing, we could not live. Our lives depend on God's re-encountering us again and again, making us alive over and over. This is what it means to live by grace. We live by the grace of God, God's breath. It's a lot to ask us to believe. It seems both unlikely and unscientific. It's almost enough to make us not believe, to think that this is actually what we are asked to believe.

Israel and Judah were asked to believe this. And they pretty much didn't. Who can blame them? Yet their lack of belief is the root of the problem in all these stories over and over and over again. The people quit believing that life depends on God and believe it depends on other things. They don't have that much science, but still, they can't believe it. Or keep forgetting it, and that's what the book of Ezekiel is about: "The only ground of hope is the presence of God in the life of [humanity]."[6]

Ezekiel tells the story with some pretty unusual metaphors, ones that seem like they might be out of bounds.

Ezekiel depicts God pretty graphically as Jerusalem's lover. God says, "I . . . saw you weltering in your blood, I said to you in your blood, 'Live, and grow up. . . .' And you grew up and became tall and arrived at full maidenhood; your breasts were formed, and your hair had grown; yet you were naked and bare" (Ezekiel 16:6–7). She's at the age for love, Ezekiel says, and so God spreads God's robe over her nakedness and plights God's troth to her. Then God says, "And you became mine" (Ezekiel 16:8). And God bathes her and anoints her with oil and swaths her in linen. God gives her delightful things to wear and eat and a beautiful place to live. God gives her life, and she grows exceedingly lovely. She becomes renowned for her beauty.

Then Jerusalem begins to trust in her beauty. She forgets her lover who gave her the life and the beauty. And she takes all the goodness, all the beauty, the fair jewels God has given her, and she makes images out of them. And she "plays the harlot" with the idols: she makes love to them. She has sex with the idols. And then she starts taking the oil God anointed her with and the bread and the honey God fed her with, and she places it all before the idols. She even takes the children that God gave her, and she sacrifices them to the idols. She gives them to the idols to be devoured, and she doesn't even remember God.

I didn't hear these particular metaphors in Sunday school, but they work pretty well on me. They make me want to cry. They seem to describe something that happens again and again. We generally don't believe anything about living by the breath of God. We believe in all sorts of other things —money and power and fame and the names that we make for ourselves—and we make love to our idols. We sacrifice everything to them because we believe in them, yet what we believe in doesn't seem to generate life. It seems to generate water parks and TV and ambition and money and McDonald's and anxiety and violence. It destroys real relationship and the wilderness and all sorts of possibility. And we sacrifice our children to the idols. Sacrifice our children to things without life. That's what makes me want to cry. What if our kids believe in money and power? How can they not? Of course they will. I do. And I think our belief might be darkness and death.

Israel made deals, gave its life, believed its life and security were in the empire of idols. The people of God believed in the tower, in the system. They believed that by working the system they would become a great nation, and it didn't work out so well for them. The people are in exile in Babylon. The nation is divided. The great Promised Land, the life, the flowing milk and honey dried up, and the book of Ezekiel dramatically climaxes in this valley where the nation has become a heap of dry bones, a huge pile of death. There is no possibility of life. The people quit longing, forgot to long, and they followed the grid plan and did the system and made love to idols that were not alive. And their flesh and blood and hearts and brains and veins and eyes and ears dried up. And there are just dry bones. No life. Just strip malls and parking lots and Applebee's and Motel 6 and coloring books and cable TV and thirty thousand Mary-Kate and Ashley products; and bombed-out buildings, lies, propaganda, and not very many questions and nothing but PR. Marketing has replaced the blood that used to run through our veins, and the marrow in our bones has dried up.

And God asks Ezekiel, "Can these bones live?" And the obvious answer is no. But God actually tells Ezekiel to say to the bones, "Dry bones, hear the word of the LORD." It's a little bit funny. I mean, sort of, don't you think—talking to bones? How are they supposed to hear? With their ears? They don't have ears. They are *bones*. But God keeps pushing.

God says, "I'm going to breathe into the bones and they'll live." God says to the bones, "I will lay sinews upon you, and will cause flesh to come upon you, and cover you with skin," and give you back your nerve endings and senses, your ears and nostrils. Can you imagine watching that? God comes up close and puts God's mouth on their nostrils and breathes into them and they live.

It doesn't sound like what God does is somehow to nurture the spiritual life of the bones. It doesn't sound like the life God has to do with here is metaphorical or metaphysical. It sounds like the bones get flesh and muscles and skin and senses by the grace of God.

What if we live—really, in every single way—by the grace of God? What if it's God who blows air into our throats and makes us breathe and feel hunger and anger and sadness and love? The thought is beautiful and unbelievable and maybe a little frightening. Because if we live really by the grace of God, depending on God's mercy, then if God withdraws, there is no more life. What we proclaim in the church is that God doesn't withdraw, ever. Even when we're bone. Even when it looks like the marrow has all been sucked out and there's nothing left but idols. Even when we don't know it or believe it or want it or have any idea about it, even when we are entirely incapable of seeing, God is close, breathing life into our throats. God continually, intimately, encounters us. God is breathing out life everywhere, all the time. I think being really alive might be like living in constant gratitude for God's breath, rather than grasping or fearing or worrying or making love to idols. But even if we can't make ourselves remember that, the Breather breathes.

7

Two Mule-Loads of Dirt

Naaman, commander of the army of the king of Syria, was a great man with his master and in high favor, because by him the LORD had given victory to Syria. He was a mighty man of valor, but he was a leper. Now the Syrians on one of their raids had carried off a little maid from the land of Israel, and she waited on Naaman's wife. She said to her mistress, "Would that my lord were with the prophet who is in Samaria! He would cure him of his leprosy." So Naaman went in and told his lord, "Thus and so spoke the maiden from the land of Israel." And the king of Syria said, "Go now, and I will send a letter to the king of Israel."

So he went, taking with him ten talents of silver, six thousand shekels of gold, and ten festal garments. And he brought the letter to the king of Israel, which read, "When this letter reaches you, know that I have sent to you Naaman my servant, that you may cure him of his leprosy." And when the king of Israel read the letter, he rent his clothes and said, "Am I God, to kill and to make alive, that this man sends word to me to cure a man of his leprosy? Only consider, and see how he is seeking a quarrel with me."

But when Elisha the man of God heard that the king of Israel had rent his clothes, he sent to the king, saying, "Why have you rent your clothes? Let him come now to me, that he may know that there is a prophet in Israel." So Naaman came with his horses and chariots, and halted at the door of Elisha's house. And Elisha sent a messenger to him, saying, "Go and wash in the Jordan seven times, and your flesh shall be restored, and you shall be clean." But Naaman was angry, and went away, saying, "Behold, I thought that he would surely come out to me, and stand, and call on the name of the LORD his God, and wave his hand over the place, and cure the leper. Are not Abana and Pharpar, the rivers of Damascus, better than all the waters of Israel? Could I not wash in them, and be clean?" So he turned and went away in a rage. But his servants came near and said to him, "My father, if the prophet had commanded you to do some great thing, would you not have done it? How much rather, then, when he says to you, 'Wash, and be clean'?" So he went down and dipped himself seven times in the Jordan, according to the word of the man of God; and his flesh was restored like the flesh of a little child, and he was clean.

Then he returned to the man of God, he and all his company, and he came and stood before him; and he said, "Behold, I know that there is no God in all the earth but in Israel; so accept now a present from your servant." But he said, "As the LORD lives, whom I serve, I will receive none." And he urged him to take it, but he refused. Then Naaman said, "If not, I pray you, let there be given to your servant two mules' burden of earth; for henceforth your servant will not offer burnt offering or sacrifice to any god but the LORD. In this matter may the LORD pardon your servant: when my master goes into the house of Rimmon to worship there, leaning on my arm, and I bow myself in the house of Rimmon, when I bow myself in the house of Rimmon, the

LORD pardon your servant in this matter." He said to him, "Go in peace."

2 Kings 5:1–19

Sometimes you're reading the Bible and it's not at all surprising, plodding and plodding like some rhythm is being established, something practically formulaic, and you begin to glaze over because it's going to be entirely predictable, and then every once in a while you find napalm smeared unexpectedly on some page in Deuteronomy, or Leviticus, or in the fifth chapter of the second book of Kings. And if it's lit, the flames blaze and the sparks scatter and land in Matthew and James and Revelation, and the whole thick book reverberates from the explosion.

Jesus just mentions the story of Naaman one day in the synagogue, and all the people suddenly fly into a rage and drag him to a cliff to hurl him to his death. Jesus says, "There were many lepers in Israel in the time of the prophet Elisha, and none of them was cleansed, but only Naaman the Syrian," and the synagogue explodes (Luke 4:27–30).

Naaman made his living by violence, and particularly (since he was a general in Syria, and Syria was perpetually at war with Israel) by violence against the people of God. Warfare was not remote and electronic in those days. Most likely Naaman gained his position, his honor, his prestige, by hacking people to death with his sword. Naaman was not someone without status, someone shunned from the community, someone in need of acceptance and a warm embrace—he was the enemy.

The story presses *outsider* as far as outsider can be pressed. If bloody-warmaker-on-the-people-of-God was not enough, he also had this other problem: a little swelling, big white scabs, flaking skin, sort of like fungus or mildew. He was a leper. Strangely, this seems to have had little effect on his social life, his place in society. Perhaps he wore makeup, turtlenecks, or drapey hoods. Maybe he had a way of covering his face so that his shame was concealed.

Kings is a book about big things. It's about the nation of Israel in a time of political crisis, in a time of war. It's about battles and politics. But here, in the story of Naaman, the narrative cuts away from all that bigness to this very little story about a problem the enemy is having with his skin.

Maybe occasionally at home, in private, Naaman would get rid of the hood and the turtleneck, put on a T-shirt, and stretch out on the couch, oblivious to his vulnerability. Maybe that's how it happened one day that the slave girl from Israel was so bold to speak. Maybe she saw him like that and was so surprised and grossed out that she couldn't help but exclaim, "My God, that man should do something about his skin! Would that my lord were with the prophet in Samaria! He would cure him of his leprosy."

The book of Kings has almost entirely to do with kings, with the ruling class, with politics. It's about history-making, world-changing, significant events. It gets everyone looking to the people who have made names for themselves. But suddenly the author changes the scene, takes us to Naaman's living room. This whole story (the napalm, the fire) is set in motion by the little words of an insignificant girl whose name is not even recorded.

This story apparently has no large effects. Not world peace: Syria goes to war with Israel in the next chapter, and Naaman probably leads the forces. We never hear of any of these people again, and there are no heroes. The little girl says, "Go to Israel." And strangely, Naaman listens. He goes to his king, and the king of Syria says, "Go to the king of Israel. I will write a letter that explains what you want." And Naaman is off.

When at last he's rounding the bend to the Israelite palace, the king of Israel glances out his window. He sees the Syrian colors flying, and every paranoid bone in his body comes alive. He runs this way and that; he bites his nails; he thinks he might vomit. He pulls himself together and answers the door. He is handed a letter: "When this letter reaches you, know that I have sent my man Naaman to you, that you may cure him of his leprosy." The king shrieks. He flings himself on the floor. He rends his clothes, and he cries, "Am I God? I can't heal this man. Why are they picking a fight with me, making an excuse for war?"

The king lives in a political world, and this is all he has eyes for. He has lived in the tower so long that he can't see outside of it. He is ostensibly the leader of God's people, but he is so enmeshed in the political that he is blind to any trace of God. His is a world of strategic planning, diplomatic posturing, public relations. His concern for the health of the institution, the expansion of the kingdom, is all consuming. It has ceased to occur to him that God might work entirely outside of this realm.

So Elisha the prophet steps in. His sight is different from the king's. Like all prophets, he stands outside the formal structures, the institution, what consumes the king. He knows immediately that the Syrian's visit isn't about power or politics or nations. He sees Naaman. And he says to the king, "Why have you rent your clothes? Let him come to me."

Whenever Elisha appears in this book almost entirely about politics, you can invariably expect something different, some sort of intimate encounter. He brings a friend's dead little boy to life, he helps a widow pay her rent, he feeds people and gives them water. At times he takes on legendary, mythical qualities, like some mysterious wood gnome. He's the bald-headed wizard that the bears avenge.

Naaman shows up at Elisha's with a whole entourage bearing gifts, and Elisha, in the ultimate of insults, doesn't even go to the door. He sends out his helper to say (without as much as a polite greeting), "Go and bathe seven times in the Jordan, and you shall be healed." Naaman is outraged. Dip seven times in a muddy little river? How arbitrary. Where's the ceremony? The holy man? The shaman? Where's the drama? He wants some incantations, some waving of the hands, some attention. Did he come all the way to Israel to get in the stupid puny muddy shallow little river? He could have bathed in the gorgeous mountain rivers of Damascus.

What Elisha says will heal him seems absurd, senseless, worthless. It is so not big. How could it be the word of God? Naaman stalks off in a rage. He refuses to do it. He refused to believe there could be healing in this nothing, in this small, insignificant act.

"But his servants came forward and spoke to him." And again the action of this story is propelled in a most unlikely way. These minor characters, these men without names, approach Naaman, who is so furious and so resolute, and they say, "Uh, excuse me, but you came all this way. Maybe it won't help, but it couldn't hurt. Why don't you just try getting in the water?" These words aren't very compelling or faithful or filled with power, but Naaman listens, and he gets in the water. And he is healed. He is made whole. His flesh becomes like a little boy's.

In the vast medley of private and public actions and political and economic decisions, in the enormous and incomprehensible complexity of the history of the world, some decisions—some insignificant words and small deeds—perform the word of God.[1] In the swarming, proliferating incoherence of humanity, God moves. God follows insignificant, inadequate human paths in order to touch and to heal and to reconcile humanity to Godself. In this little muddy river, Naaman finds that his shame is washed away.

He is grateful. He is moved. He returns to Elisha and declares his conversion. He says, "Now I know that there is no god in the whole world except the god of Israel." And he presses Elisha to accept gifts for his gratitude. But Elisha refuses. Naaman looks around, doesn't quite know what to do next, and finally says, "Okay, look then, I'm going back to Syria, where this god is not worshiped. Let me take two mule-loads of your dirt so I can build an altar to the God of Israel, because from now on, I will worship no other god."

He continues rambling, "Of course, except, pardon me for this, but when I go back to Syria, and I go into the house of my master's god, Rimmon, and the king leans on my arm, so that I bow down to Rimmon, okay, when *I* bow down in the temple of Rimmon, may the Lord pardon me."

Some conversion. One minute he says he's going to be loyal to God, and the next minute he's making some convoluted apology for his intention to continue worshiping an idol. This is not the sort of conversion that draws a great deal of admiration. This is not renouncing idolatry to "hang suspended." Sure, Naaman was happy that his leprosy was gone, but clearly his ideas about God are all wrong. He thinks carrying around two mule-loads of earth will make God available to him.

Naaman's the worst. He's all wrong. Really all wrong. He's *so* the enemy. He kills people. He makes war. He's a bad theologian. He's crabby and irritable and self-important and arrogant, getting so enraged when he's not treated like he thinks he should be. He's a liar and a blatant idol worshiper.

If this story were in line with the rest of the book of Kings, which is one big long intensive polemic against idolatry— which is really one big long intensive rant against anybody bowing down to any other god but the God of Israel—well, this is the point in the story where the prophet's fury would be unleashed, or the leprosy would sprout back and consume Naaman. Or he'd be slaughtered by the sword like all the other pagan sympathizers in the book of Kings.

You can't say, "I will serve no other god but Yahweh," and *immediately* after that say, "I'm going to bow down to an idol." Can you?

The book of Kings is a story of the nation of Israel, God's people. It ends horribly. The kingdom is totally demolished; the people are left without a home; the land God promised them is lost. It is the nadir of horrible events in their history. The person who wrote Kings is trying to make sense of the catastrophe. When the people moved into the Promised Land they were drawn to the "high places" of the gods of the land. The book is a fury of intolerance for this activity. The people were not faithful to God, they accommodated to idols, and they lost the land. Every king in Kings is judged solely on this criterion: did he accommodate? And most are condemned. The most furious rhetoric, the bloodiest intolerance, is directed at those who worship Baal, the Canaanite god of thunder. Rimmon is the Syrian god of thunder. It is to him that Naaman admits he will bow down.

Everything in the context of this book would have us expect that the mere hint of such a suggestion would bring down the prophet's fury. But Elisha hears his confession and says, "Go in peace." This is not simply "Farewell." This is not "Get out of here, you sniveling pagan." It is a benediction. It means, "You are entirely embraced by the love of God; go in peace."

Maybe Naaman's confession is somehow the truest confession, embracing the conflict or contradiction or tension inherent in faith in God. You can't serve God and mammon.

But we will. Naaman knows he will. We do it incessantly. I do. We are going to bow down to the gods of our world, our ideologies, our theologies, the gods our nations create. We're going to serve money or power or glory or righteousness or capitalism or revolution or socialism or anarchism or cynicism. We are going to fix something in our gaze, plant it in soil, believe in it, and cling to it. And the world's going to be a bloody mess because we're all bowing down all the time, making wars over those idols and believing they are gods.

Not only is Naaman the enemy of God's people, not only does he have their blood on his hands, he asks permission to be excused for bowing down to an idol, and Elisha pronounces to him the word of the Lord, "Go in peace. You are reconciled." The agenda of the book of Kings is subverted. Elisha offers no ethical advice, no rules or regulations, no methods for ridding his life of the worship of Rimmon. He has no solution to propose. "Yet he does not let him go away empty."[2] With utter generosity, he grants him the freedom to rest in the peace of God. This is God's word to Naaman, and I hear in it a blessing for the whole tangle of the human condition.

Flesh

8

The Ultimate Anti-Idolatry Story

And the Word became flesh and dwelt among us, full of
grace and truth.

John 1:14

Absolute paradox

The Christian story is not exactly abounding in scientifically
verifiable details. In fact, it makes a few claims that seem
almost absurd, slightly irrational—for instance, its central
claim, that the Word became flesh and dwelt among us. If
that meant some divine spark resides within humanity, it
would seem less preposterous, but what it means is that
God became a human being. What it means is that God got
a nose and a mouth and feet. That's a weird and vaguely
embarrassing thing to uphold.

It's no wonder that there are always plenty of smart people in the Christian church who want to distance themselves from this claim. It seems like claiming it as the truth puts you in the category of fool or prehistoric person or unscientific superstitious person who believes in fairies and ghosts and the danger of black cats crossing your path. A god taking human form—it's good material for a myth. Gods transmute into all sorts of interesting things. Loki the jealous, in Norse legend, takes the shape of an old woman in order to discover the mistletoe that will kill his rival. The god Sakka, in a legend from India, comes down from his cloud to see if the hare is really willing to give himself as a sacrifice to a hungry creature. Isis becomes a swallow and a giant perch. I'm a little bit embarrassed to admit it, but I like watching movies where mutant beings morph back and forth from ordinary humans to Wolverine Man or Electric Woman, superpower people. It must be an inherently potent idea, suggesting all sorts of things about human greatness and human limitation and the powers we struggle with, because it's been done a million times in myths and folktales and comic books. But I don't think anyone even tries to believe these stories in the way Christians believe in Jesus Christ. Our faith is not something that is founded particularly on sensibleness.

Susan Handelman in her book *Slayers of Moses* suggests that the church seized on "the Word became flesh," made it a necessary doctrine, because it reduced the complexity of interpretation. Instead of the ceaseless multiplicity of the rabbis reading and rereading the word (words, words everywhere without clear referents, words that could be struggled over, fought with), the Word become flesh was one Word, and one Word only. The Word become flesh made a neater package. Jesus Christ helped to pin a few things down. If he was the one true answer, the clear referent for every word in the Bible,

108

the absolute and ultimate signified, then that seemed rather to simplify things. Now, at last, there need be no more of the messy plurality, unmanageability, unknowability. She says, "Instead of the ceaseless play of interpretation, the Church Fathers needed to articulate dogma, and did not tolerate plurality and difference lightly."[1] This, she says, has defined the Christian relationship to the text. "The Word became flesh" became a means to limit all that uncontrollable articulation. Now there was one right way to read.

It's funny that this should happen or appear to happen, because "the Word became flesh," the story of Jesus Christ, is not a story that seems to exactly promote conceptual clarity. The Christian story is that God reveals Godself not as a rational system or a set of laws or an ideal or idea or a spirituality or an unchanging principle or the platonic ideal or even metaphysical being itself, not as something less outrageous than life, but as a man, Jesus Christ. A living man. With cells and bones and a urinary tract. Flesh. Not a rock, not at all. That God would reveal Godself in this surprising and familiar way seems like it might give birth to more unruly ponderings and articulations than it would put to rest.

The incarnation is not something you can believe in like you can believe in the solution to an equation or dinosaurs or penicillin or the US victory in Iwo Jima. The incarnation is the foundation of our faith, and yet you can hardly think clearly enough about it to begin to comprehend it. You can look at it and look at it and still never get it in focus. It's blurry and puzzling and enigmatic and inapprehensible. Unsystematizable. If it is somehow the greatest truth, the most important revelation, it's not something you can grasp. Kierkegaard called the central tenet of Christianity, that God became a human being, an absolute paradox. It's not something you "get" through reason; it's something that challenges reason. It doesn't fit into a logical system.

Flesh

I've been asking people what they think of when they hear the word *flesh*; not whether they like it or not, but what they believe it suggests in the context of the Bible. Almost unanimously, people say something along the lines of "our base animal nature," "the naughty human impulses," "lust," "animal desire," "sexual sin." Though my polling techniques were not methodical (okay, I only polled maybe ten people), I think I covered a fairly broad range: my atheist cousin, my evangelical Christian father, my Eastern Orthodox sister, my Buddhist-leaning husband, and my super-liberal vaguely spiritual brother (okay, they were all related to me, but still). I think it's fair to say that their responses represent a pretty widespread perception about what flesh denotes in the Bible. You don't have to poll anyone; you just need to recognize the general vibe. People both inside and outside of the church often have the impression that Christianity is all about the struggle between our flesh (our animal desires) and our spirit (our, I guess, better-behaved desires).

I think we got this impression about the flesh from Christian preachers or Sunday-school teachers or reading Paul. It's funny, though, because when I searched the Internet for what people are saying and writing about flesh in the Bible, I found hundreds of sermons and seminary papers from all sorts of places—Peninsula Bible College, Berean Bible Church, fundamentalist and evangelical sounding places, hardly a libertine among them—and they all argued that flesh does not mean what we all seem to think it means. When Paul says flesh, he doesn't mean our bad bodies. If what he means can be construed as "naughty desire," it isn't our naughty desire for sex, it is our naughty desire for legalism and the law and all the things humanity comes to depend on other than the grace of God.

Bondage to the flesh, for Paul, was living locked in the realm of alienation. Living there might lead you to Paul's lists of bads ("fornication, impurity, licentiousness, idolatry, sorcery, enmity, strife, jealousy, anger, selfishness, dissension, party spirit, envy, drunkenness, carousing, and the like," Galatians 5:19–21), but it isn't particularly bodily lust that leads you, it's living in contradiction to the love and mercy God intends. Living in the realm of alienation leads you to things that break community rather than to things that make love.

I don't like the word *naughty*. I don't like how it sounds. It bothers me when I hear parents say it to their children. Maybe my grandmother or my parents used it too much on me and I have some sort of deep-seated rebellion to the category. I especially dislike it when it's used in the context of sin. It seems so reductive, like a category made up by parents who don't want their children to get dirty, or a category made up by adolescent boys who spend too much time in their bedrooms with magazines. It may be that the boys are dwelling in the realm of alienation, but we need far deeper and thicker and serious words to describe the realm of alienation from life. Sin is not being naughty. Sin is serving death.

The Word became flesh

Karl Barth says, and this seems huge to me, "The conflict of man," the tension, is not between animal baseness and human greatness, it is between "total freedom and total bondage."² Christ doesn't come to help us achieve our goals, but to ease the nooses from our necks, to loose the ropes that are choking the life of the world, to reveal the God of life.

The Gospel of John talks about life a lot. John says that to receive what Jesus brings is to pass "from death to life" (5:24). He says "in him was life, and the life was the light of [humanity]" (1:4). He says Jesus comes "that [we] may have life, and have it abundantly" (10:10). He talks about eternal life, and he doesn't mean by that the infinite duration of the disembodied soul. He talks about eating and drinking life. He talks about it like it's water that wells up continually and quenches thirst, something vigorous and flourishing, wholly adequate and lush. God didn't become flesh to institute a religion that condemns sexuality or decries the physical world, but to free us from our attachment to what is not alive, what is death, what doesn't feed us but drains us of life.

When John says "the Word became flesh," he means something more than that God took on the form of a human, something different from Loki changing shape to find the mistletoe. God "did not merely bear the body . . . [God] chose for [God] self all the deep poverty of the cosmic impotence and limitation of fleshly being."³ God becomes vulnerable in Jesus Christ in an unmistakable way.

But it doesn't seem like, for John, the vulnerability necessarily starts with the child at the manger. John doesn't start his story there, he goes way, way, way back to the very beginning, to the genesis of all things, and he says that the Word was there, in the bosom of God. He claims that the world was made through this Word. God loved the world into being. The Word was the life of humanity, but humans didn't recognize it, didn't let it in. They let in a lot of other things: Seinfeld, the Power Rangers, Oprah, and Bill

O'Reilly. They found all sorts of other ways to try to get life: dancing around statues, tapping keyboards, making love to idols. But with the Word they would not socialize.

But the Word didn't retreat, didn't withdraw to the heart of God. Of course it didn't—retreat isn't in God's heart. The Word was God's yearning to be with creation, to nurture it, to be intimately connected with it. And though it is constantly rebuffed by humanity, it doesn't retreat. Instead it goes an inconceivable distance in the opposite direction. It takes on everything we are, our DNA, our lymphatic system. God is not put off by all our alienating behavior. God doesn't turn up God's nose at the tapping and the dancing and the idolmaking, doesn't retreat to the confines of the pure and unsullied air of the castle conservatory. Instead God is determined to overcome the alienation, at apparently whatever cost.

"The Word became flesh" is God acting, God reaching. It reveals the lengths God is willing to go in pursuit of humanity, and it reveals an intimate, passionate, and vulnerable pursuit. The Word enters the darkness in order to bring light. Barth says that in this act "the antithesis, the distance, the abstraction that is created by the fact of darkness . . . is overcome."[4] It was not God who created the distance: it was humanity; it was sin. And in Jesus Christ, the distance is overcome.

Jesus Christ isn't God standing back, beckoning fools to get out of their big and loud and stinky vehicles; Jesus is God climbing in the seat beside the fools and remaining there for the duration of the ride. The Word become flesh isn't God giving up and turning away in disgust when God sees the people eat their third meal of the week from McDonald's; it is God joining them for the meal. Instead of God protecting God's good reputation, remaining above all the futility of the human race, instead of God maintaining good taste and impeccable manners, in Jesus we see God entering the paltry ruckus of life as we know it. It looks foolish. But it reveals, perhaps, something about how God feels about us. It was always in God's heart to give up glory and power in order to achieve union. In the story John tells, wisdom plays the fool in order to be with us. The story of the Word become flesh is the story of God with us in an incredibly vulnerable way.

Christians claim that God's fullest revelation of Godself is Jesus Christ. Through Jesus Christ we can know (but of course "know" here means something different from "comprehend") God. Karl Barth was super-adamant about saying that the entire content of the Bible points to Jesus Christ. He even says some outrageous things like this: "The Bible says all sorts of things, certainly; but in all this multiplicity and variety, it says in truth only one thing—just this; the name of Jesus Christ."[5] At first blush this looks like the deadening sort of move of some idolatrous foundationalist—like what Susan Handelman accused the church of doing—but I think it is actually just the opposite. Because what Barth means by this is absolutely not to point to something static; he means to point to something at the heart of Christian faith that is alive and ungraspable, something that would deconstruct every idol humans could build. At the center is not a dogmatic claim but something thoroughly relational, Emmanuel, God-with-us. And Barth points to Christ so adamantly not out of some sort of dogmatic desire to convert the world, but because what Christ reveals is that the Christian message is unalloyed good news. In Christ, God's holiness reveals itself as God having mercy on us, God's omnipotence reveals itself as the weakness of Jesus on the cross, God's justice reveals itself as Christ's identification of himself with our unrighteousness. Barth's theology points to Jesus Christ, the Word of God, because he believes Jesus is the best Word that can be said. And this Word can't arise from within us; it is given us by our relationship to the Other. For Barth the revelation inevitably causes a crisis, but it is also the greatest possible hope.

That the Word became living, breathing flesh would seem to make it apparent that knowing God, believing in God, is not like giving your life to some abstract truth, something static. It would seem to make it apparent that believing in God isn't like possessing some secret knowledge, or assenting to some intellectual truth, or knowing four spiritual laws. To know and believe in God is to be immersed in the complexity of relationship—more like knowing someone who loves you, likes you, pursues you doggedly than like knowing something or achieving something. The idea that our most significant struggle in life is between our human nature and some higher ideal is a lie, it seems to me, that is overcome by the incarnation. It is not this false dualism that God comes to sort out, but rather our alienation from the source of life and love.

9

The Mother of God

In those days Mary arose and went with haste into the hill country, to a city of Judah, and she entered the house of Zechariah and greeted Elizabeth. And when Elizabeth heard the greeting of Mary, the babe leaped in her womb; and Elizabeth was filled with the Holy Spirit and she exclaimed with a loud cry, "Blessed are you among women, and blessed is the fruit of your womb! And why is this granted me, that the mother of my Lord should come to me? For behold, when the voice of your greeting came to my ears, the babe in my womb leaped for joy. And blessed is she who believed that there would be a fulfillment of what was spoken to her from the Lord."

Luke 1:39–46

The story of the church for two thousand years has been that God was born from a woman's womb. However creedal the virgin birth has become, it's actually enough to make you whirl or stagger or fall down or jump up; more supercalifragilisticexpialidocious than the tepid routine of Christmas pageants might lead one to believe. It's an audacious claim: God was formed in the womb of a woman, and even more, without the help of a man. Though set in a male-dominated culture, the story of Christ's birth involves no male seed. At all. God grew bones and flesh from Mary's cells and blood. It is in his mother's womb that God becomes human. It's not by the "will of man" that God is conceived, which, as *The New Interpreter's Bible* points out, means that sperm has no role.[1]

Patriarchy, strictly defined, is a system of social organization that traces everything—lineage, ancestry, inheritance—through the male line. Passing on the male seed is crucial. Through it you get your honor, your status, your proper place in the hierarchy, your power. The Christmas story (the story of the virgin birth) may not be really overt about subverting patriarchy, but subversion is embedded in the story because there is no male seed. It's weird that Matthew and Luke trace Jesus' genealogy through Joseph, but I wonder if that was like a hidden joke, or a vast oversight, or if they were just trying to make some concession to convention, because you can't really trace the trail of the male seed when there is no male seed involved. Jesus Christ, the Son of God, has no male blood lineage. That seems to throw a bit of a kink into the whole patriarchy thing. Not to denigrate the male seed, but you have to admit it takes some of the limelight off the phallus as the embodiment of generative power.

For some reason, what the church has most often emphasized about the virgin birth is that it doesn't involve the physical act of sex. But the story of God coming into the world is really astoundingly physical. The incarnation involves a fetus in a uterus passing through a cervix in a process (if you can really even quite call it a process) that involves sweating and blood and amniotic fluid and a placenta. If you've ever grown a baby in your womb and birthed it, you might have an idea of what it means to say that God became incarnate in this manner. That it was a virgin birth doesn't mean it was neat and clean and polite and somehow spiritual as opposed to physical; it means that it didn't involve the male seed.

Possibly this is just emasculating enough that it has been a little hard for the church to concentrate on.

Matthew manages to make his story about Christ's conception and birth as much about men as possible under the circumstances. He can't ultimately leave the women out, but he seems to give it his best shot. Matthew says Mary is found to be pregnant. He doesn't tell us anything about her reaction to this, but he has an angel appear to Joseph to explain to him what's going on and to urge him not to divorce her. The whole deal seems to be worked out in proper patriarchal fashion, without consulting Mary. Luke tells the story from a pretty different angle. In Luke's story, the angel comes to Mary and tells her that she has been chosen to give birth to the savior. Mary doesn't say, "Why thank you, allow me to speak with my fiancé, Joseph, about this." She immediately runs to the house of her cousin Elizabeth, who, according to the angel, is also mysteriously pregnant.

Elizabeth was old and had been called barren. It must have felt like there was suddenly an explosion of unexplainable fertility. Their meeting is not really quite the scene you might expect in a patriarchal society. The unwed mother doesn't go submissively to her man to gently try to explain the apparent scandal, as a proper member of a patriarchal system might or should. Instead, she runs off to celebrate fertility with her pregnant sister friend.

119

In the fifteenth century the scenario might have been enough to get Mary and Elizabeth burned at the stake. The unwed mother who is mysteriously pregnant meets with the old crone who, miraculously, is also pregnant, and together they revel in the fruit of their wombs. They might as well have let their hair down, burned incense, and danced naked by the light of the full moon. But this isn't actually a record of a meeting of a pagan fertility cult. It isn't part of the vast array of noncanonical writing. It's the Gospel of Luke. It's where the Catholic Church got some of the words for the Hail Mary. It's iconic. It's orthodox. It's read in fundamentalist households everywhere. And it's so, I don't know, voluptuous. The church might have heard something sweet and submissive in these stories of the pregnant women, but there are flashes that dazzle and sizzle.

The story is thick with sensuality. Inside the women's bodies, the bones of God and the bones of John the Baptist are being knit. Mary and Elizabeth are preparing for the advent of Christ, at least in part, like all pregnant women prepare for birth. They eat more, their bodies change, their breasts fill. Soon God will be sucking voraciously at his mother's breast.

When Mary runs up and greets Elizabeth, Elizabeth feels a movement deep inside her pelvic region. This is the indication that the Messiah is present, that the divine has been recognized. Not some rational observation, but a flutter in the belly. John the Baptist is best known as the figure that calls people to prepare the way of the Lord. He is the witness to the Word. He never seems like much of a particularly rational, contained sort of figure, and his witness is never exactly systematic, but here it's especially nonarticulate. This is the story of the first time the first one recognized God incarnate. It's not some smart theologian—it's not Karl Barth or the pope or a mystic or a holy guy or a prayer warrior—it's a preconscious, preverbal fetus floating in amniotic fluid. He responds to the sound of the voice of God's mother and leaps for joy in his mother's womb. Usually I think of John the Baptist as older and hairier and scarier, a little bit terse and grumpy. But I like thinking of him here as a baby, making his first prophetic movement, nonarticulate, nonverbal, and unambiguously joyful.

Like little John the Baptist in Luke's story, we first meet Jesus Christ in utero. God was truly made flesh in Mary's womb. This is not a pagan invention. It's at the heart of orthodox Christian doctrine. That seems beautiful to me, and strange. It seems like Protestants don't really think about Mary the mother of God that much. They are cautious about venerating her unduly because it's idolatrous or cultish, or just too kitschy, or theologically suspect. But maybe they also are cautious to avoid confronting too palpably the fleshly, human Jesus. Here God is so obviously made flesh. Thinking about Mary makes us think about that. God comes into the world as a baby. Naked and needy. That's the way the Christian story goes. That's a significant revelation. And it's maybe not all that comfortable for us. God doesn't come to the world looking big and self-sufficient and simple and coherent, like an answer or a moral absolute, but looking weak and hungry, totally dependent on his mother. That's what babies are like. They can't propel themselves. They can't even focus their eyes. *Helpless* is not a bad word for what a baby is. God comes into the world as a baby. That is a subversion of how we might expect the almighty God to come.

This hasn't always immediately struck everyone as good news. Ever since people heard this story, there's been a tendency to think it might be better to have a God that never really shared the weakness of the flesh. A God that never really shared our weakness, our blood, our bones, our need. But whenever that tendency surfaced, the community looked back over everything and said, you can't get away from it. The Christian story is a story about God become human: fully human, fully God. You may choose another story, but then it's not this one.

We might prefer a story about a god that comes to lift us out of our complicated, fleshly, sometimes beautiful, sometimes incredibly painful humanness. The startling Christmas revelation is that we get a God who comes to us flesh and blood, human and vulnerable, a baby born from between his mother's legs and set in a trough that animals are fed from, of all things. Sweet Mary, mother of God.

10

A Pathological Attraction to Revolutionaries

And as he sat at table in his house, many tax collectors and sinners were sitting with Jesus and his disciples; for there were many who followed him. And the scribes of the Pharisees, when they saw that he was eating with sinners and tax collectors, said to his disciples, "Why does he eat with tax collectors and sinners?" And when Jesus heard it, he said to them, "Those who are well have no need of a physician, but those who are sick; I came not to call the righteous, but sinners."

Now John's disciples and the Pharisees were fasting; and people came and said to him, "Why do John's disciples and the disciples of the Pharisees fast, but your disciples do not fast?" And Jesus said to them, "Can the wedding guests fast while the bridegroom is with them? As long as they have the bridegroom with them, they cannot fast. The days will come, when the bridegroom is taken away from them, and then they will fast in that day. No one sews a piece of unshrunk cloth on an old garment; if he does, the patch tears away from it, the new from the old, and a worse tear is made. And no one puts new wine into old wineskins; if he does, the wine will burst the skins, and the wine is lost, and so are the skins; but new wine is for fresh skins."

One sabbath he was going through the grainfields; and as they made their way his disciples began to pluck heads of grain. And the Pharisees said to him, "Look, why are they doing what is not lawful on the sabbath?" And he said to them, "Have you never read what David did, when he was in need and was hungry, he and those who were with him: how he entered the house of God, when Abiathar was high priest, and ate the bread of the Presence, which it is not lawful for any but the priests to eat, and also gave it to those who were with him?" And he said to them, "The sabbath was made for man, not man for the sabbath; so the Son of man is lord even of the sabbath."

Mark 2:15–28

I like Fidel Castro. This offends my father, and he can readily outline fifty thousand reasons why I shouldn't. But I can't help it. I have a nearly pathological attraction to revolutionaries. Name most any revolutionary, however many awful things ended up happening in their wake, I still feel like I'd like to have dinner with them. Che Guevara, of course, but even Robespierre and—I'm sorry—even Chairman Mao. So when Jesus comes on immediately in Mark, challenging the powers that be, and I'm like oh-my-gosh-I-love-him-he's-everything-I-ever-wanted-in-a-god, and I love these texts, and I want to put them on a banner and wave it around in front of George Bush, I feel like I probably need to slow down a little bit.

So Jesus ate with tax collectors and sinners, people who were excluded by the structure. That seems cool, man—down

124

with the oppressive system. But actually there were some pretty understandable and good reasons why tax collectors didn't get invited to dinner. They did things that really, really hurt people. I've always imagined them as bureaucrats, bookish thin guys with high voices and glasses, that people didn't like because they had an unfortunate profession and they were nerdy and maybe a little bit weasely, but mostly I felt sorry for them. I think a lot of my feelings were formed by the song about Zaccheus, the wee little man.

It might actually be more accurate to imagine them as thugs who terrorize people and take puppies from little girls. It wasn't like they sat in offices doing paperwork. They stopped people on the street and barged into their houses to go through their stuff. Everything bought and sold in the Roman Empire could be taxed. You could be taxed for using a road or going over a bridge, and there was nothing to regulate the whole system. You might be on your way home from the market with your family, peacefully eating falafel and enjoying the cypress trees along the road, when suddenly this guy would stop you, bark orders, make you unload your pack animals, open every package, read your personal letters, and then basically take what he wanted from you, even the fruit from your hand. Tax collectors didn't get a paycheck from the Romans. They got paid by keeping some of what they took in taxes, so they'd try to take as much as they could. Basically they were extortionists who made their living stealing from the poor.

There are horrible stories. I read one account about a poverty-stricken man who ran away to escape a greedy tax collector. The tax collector detained his whole family—wife, kids, parents—and, Philo says, "beat them and insulted them and heaped every kind of ill treatment upon them," to try to get them to inform on the fugitive. When they wouldn't give

125

up any information, the tax collector "tortured their bodies with racks and wheels so as to kill them with newly invented kinds of death."[1] That might be an extreme example, but still. The word "tax" in Hebrew is *mas hakhnasah. Mas* means despise. It is what Pharaoh did to the Hebrew people when he forced them to make bricks for his buildings. They were his slaves. Tax collectors hurt people to fund the oppressive regime and line their own pockets.

So when Jesus is friendly with them and invites them along, it isn't just like, oh cool, he's so nice to people that the world excludes. It has a lot more bite than that. Who would invite the Muslim man Private Lindy England humiliated in Abu Ghraib to sit next to her at the dinner table? Jesus really isn't doing what is obviously "right." It's not like he is overturning stupid and vile laws and customs, and you'd practically have to be crazy and mean and oppressive not to be on Jesus' side. He isn't simply defying a bad rule that the bad old Pharisees used to be mean to people. Jesus actually defies what seems right. Not just what seems right to people we might think are bad, but what would seem right to us. I think that at the heart of his activity there may be an offense to anybody's sensibilities.

In Mark Jesus somehow doesn't appear to have that much regard for things that are actually enormously vital in most people's minds in order to preserve whatever social order they believe in. He is a bit reckless. He acts like someone who might actually do something like free the captives, empty the jails, invite turncoats and oppressors to his table.

Jesus says his disciples don't need to abide by the cultural customs of the day. He says you can't put new wine in old wineskins. I think sometimes Christians hear that and start thinking, Yep, those folks had some pretty bad old, uptight, rigid wineskins. *They* had bad wineskins. But *we've* got really nice new supple wineskins. Their containers were all wrong and mean, but our containers are good and nice. We've got the right containers for the wine. But I think the point may be more about the wine. The wine is spectacularly bold and alive. It's the redeeming blood that bursts the most precious containers and breaks your heart and runs scandalously, gracefully among us. That's the point. The wine is not something that fits in any container. It's so intense and big and recklessly, unmanageably redemptive.

Most people—probably all people, not just Pharisees—have boundaries they construct around themselves to order their world or to keep themselves pure or to try to help them be good. Jesus violates those constructs, divests them of any ultimate significance. That threatens the social order and anyone's internal order. Being confronted by the grace of God is often devastating. Not in a bad way, but in a way that means the container has to burst and the heart has to break.

After violating important social conventions and bursting old wineskins, Jesus goes on to break the Sabbath. This is a huge offense, and ominous. It is what gets the authorities set on destroying him. The Sabbath was an enormous and beautiful part of keeping the faith. Most of the time you just go about doing your work, but this is the time that you quit that. You stop. You look around. You remember that God created everything around you. And then God stopped. Said it was good. Loved it. So that's what you try to do.

When you quit working, quit exerting force on the world, it's more possible to remember profoundly that it's not all about your work, what you do. The Sabbath is about stopping and paying attention. Which seems like an important thing to do, but it isn't easy. So elaborate rules were created to help people to do it. There are thirty-seven categories of work that are forbidden on the Sabbath. You are not supposed to sift or spin or sort or warp or unravel. You are not supposed to wash or untie or burn or extinguish or slaughter.

The laws were meant to help you keep yourself from asserting yourself on creation, and to help you be thankful and know that God is God. They were meant to remind you that it's not necessary to constantly battle creation, to sift and sort and tie it up, but that there is a time to rest and love it. The work that's forbidden is any work in which you interfere with nature and act as if you are master over it. It is not only forbidden to make a bonfire, it is even forbidden to throw the smallest stick into a flame. You are not supposed to pluck a single blade of grass. Trapping is forbidden. "This includes capturing or restricting the freedom of any living creature. The prime example is trapping an animal. However, even catching an insect in one's hand comes under this heading," says Rabbi Aryeh Kaplan.[2]

You could think it's all sort of crazy and too much, but I can see how giving one whole day a week to doing all these things, or rather, not doing all these things, could actually change the world. All week you step on bugs, you trample grass, you ignore, change, destroy, use, exert your force all over the place. But on this day you pay attention, notice how it is without you exerting force. You pay attention to every living thing, and you allow it to live. All week long you live enslaved to doing things, asserting yourself, working it, but this is a day where you are freed to see something larger and greater than your work.

The Sabbath laws could be used in an oppressive way; the punishment for violation could be death. But I can see why people might have come to believe that it was a matter of life and death. Keeping the Sabbath generated life; breaking it generated death.

The Western Christian version of the day of rest lacks a little something. In my tradition, Sundays were all about trying to get people saved, and that process involved a lot of sorting and tying and washing and spinning. Then people would go to Wendy's or Rax or Steak 'n Shake. After lunch we all went home to watch sports on TV. That seems a little bit deathy.

It would be good for the world to have to observe the Sabbath, a day of rest where everyone tries not to exert their force on the world, and is grateful to God, and tries not to squash any life, not even bugs, and all the malls and fast-food restaurants and TVs are shut down. It seems like the world would be about a thirty-thousand-times better place.

Jesus violates the Sabbath. Plucking is one of the types of work that is forbidden, and his disciples are plucking. You can read this in a way that makes getting in trouble for plucking seem ridiculous. Or you could go deeper and recognize what it might be like to have one's most precious constructs overthrown, one's very deepest beliefs about what is right and good.

When the Pharisees cry, "Why are you doing this?" Jesus says, "Well, have you never heard what David did?"

And then he brings up this story from 1 Samuel that has nothing to do with a Sabbath violation but is a very crazy story. David, on the run from King Saul, first lies to the high priest at Nob, saying that the king actually sent him there. Then he says that he and his men are hungry, so the priest should feed them the sacred bread that no one but the priest is supposed to touch. And then the priest and his whole family are killed by the king for having given David the sacred bread! And, by the way, Jesus gets the priest's name wrong. He says it's Abiathar and it's really Ahimelech, Abiathar's father.

I mean, gol, he is offensive. Jesus doesn't get into the nitty-gritty of the story, but it's kind of a strange story to throw out there. And I'm not sure what he's saying, but it seems like he's saying something about the slippery nature of righteousness. Something like, people break the law when they're hungry, and it's okay. Something like, being alive is very complicated and an unruly messy sort of a thing that doesn't conform that well to ideals or standards, or any program, and that's okay. Laws were made for humans to live more fully. Humans weren't made for laws. Jesus seems, here, to set himself against any rigid definitions of righteousness or virtue. He challenges the constructs that serve to keep the order, as if it is life, it is humans, it is creation that he loves, not virtue or righteousness or the order.

Being on the side of the good guys against the bad guys may be appealing. Slinging my arm around Che Guevara and marching into the square against the oppressive regime sounds super-sexy. But it's not the kind of revolution Jesus undertakes. His revolution actually erases the lines that divide the righteous from the unrighteous. It doesn't turn things over once to finally put the righteous on top, it subverts whatever system comes to rest. It erases the lines we think are necessary for propriety and society and goodness.

We have a lot of good things to help us order our world and keep peace in society: laws, ethics, cultural norms. Jesus comes and messes with the foundations of culture. Not to create chaos, but to show us that God loves life, our life, us. Jesus abolishes a certain rigidity. Not because the particular perpetrators of it are bad people, but because it isn't true. It doesn't create love and life, because rigid wineskins can't contain this wine. Sabbath was made for humans, so that humans might live fully. It wasn't meant to impose something more important, something God loves more than humanity, onto humanity, as if God loved order and ethics and purity more than unruly, hungry, weedy, needy, muddled, messy, confused humans. It's a very scandalous thing to proclaim that the Sabbath was made for man, and not that man was made for the Sabbath.

God is incredibly, graciously, scandalously generous toward us and all people, not so much because God is counting on our reforming properly eventually, but because God loves us. So Jesus comes acting as if the most crucial thing is that we are all at the table with each other and with him—tax collectors and sinners and Bush and Castro and David and Lindy England and fast-food entrepreneurs and you and me and us and them, and the table is teeming with practically unbearable life.

11

Look at How You Hear

Again he began to teach beside the sea. And a very large crowd gathered about him, so that he got into a boat and sat in it on the sea; and the whole crowd was beside the sea on the land. And he taught them many things in parables, and in his teaching he said to them: "Listen! A sower went out to sow. And as he sowed, some seed fell along the path, and the birds came and devoured it. Other seed fell on rocky ground, where it had not much soil, and immediately it sprang up, since it had no depth of soil; and when the sun rose it was scorched, and since it had no root it withered away. Other seed fell among thorns and the thorns grew up and choked it, and it yielded no grain. And other seeds fell into good soil and brought forth grain, growing up and increasing and yielding thirtyfold and sixtyfold and a hundredfold." And he said, "He who has ears to hear, let him hear." And when he was alone, those who were about him with the twelve asked him concerning the parables. And he said to them, "To you has been given the secret of the kingdom of God, but

for those outside everything is in parables; so that they may
indeed see but not perceive, and may indeed hear but not
understand; lest they should turn again, and be forgiven."
And he said to them, "Do you not understand this parable?
How then will you understand all the parables?"

Mark 4:1–13

When I read this passage I don't feel like calling out, "Sweet
Jesus, oh dear sweet Lord." In fact, the words that go through
my mind about him are more frustrated words. I probably
shouldn't record them. It could be that I'm just generally
irritable lately, but really, even if you were coming at this
from the most nonirritable, warmly accepting place possible,
I think it would be a little bothersome.

Jesus says that he teaches in parables—speaks in obscure,
unclear, twisty sorts of ways—so that people won't understand, so that they won't get it, lest they turn and be forgiven.
That doesn't seem very nice or warm or welcoming. What
if we wrote that on a banner and put it on the doors of
our churches? It sounds like he's trying to confuse people,
intentionally being obscure and unclear. He's speaking in
opaque and perplexing ways so people won't understand.
If you get it, it's because you're somehow in. And if you
don't, well, hey, you're outside, sorry. In one sentence he
says the disciples have been given the secret, so they are in.
But in the next sentence he makes it clear they aren't, since
he spoke in a parable and they didn't get it. So he's like,
"What? You don't get it?!" It seems like he's playing with
them a little—"I guess maybe you're not in after all." They
don't understand when he speaks in parables. How will they
ever understand anything?

He goes on to explain the parable, but it's almost like his
explanation is begrudging and maybe not entirely straightforward. He doesn't really solve the puzzle, he just pretends

to. Really, he just presents another layer of words, another parable, another something that's not entirely clear. He seems to state pretty clearly that parables are intended to confuse and frustrate, so perhaps frustration is an appropriate response.

I think it would be helpful, for this moment anyway, to try to erase the pictures we have of Jesus in our minds. The ones we can hardly help having, because he's been drawn that way a million times. The ones where he is so pleasing looking, where he has that serious, kindly look on his face and a long white robe and a sheep over his shoulder, and picture instead a sort of trickster. Jim, my husband, once took Sallman's *Head of Christ* (you've probably seen the print a thousand times) from the narthex in our church and painted a jester's hat on him, floppy points with bells on the ends. He painted a harlequin outfit over the white robe and put a glint in his eye, a little bit of a mischievous look, more like "Hey, now you see it, now you don't" than Franklin Graham.

Jesus doesn't appear to be moving slowly or gently in this story. He's being a little quirky and jerky and odd and wry. Not like a logician or a mathematician or a politician; more like a joker, or a surrealist, bending things and twisting them around, "complicating what at first seemed perfectly simple, raising more problems than he solves."[1]

This is a little funny: Jesus is actually teaching the people from a boat on the sea. The text literally says, "He sat on the sea." It's an odd place to teach from. Maybe it was just practical, like some sort of organizational necessity, but Mark's really not all that big on organizational necessity, so the fact that he would even mention it makes it seem thick and potent. The people Jesus is teaching are on the solid ground, and Jesus sits on the sea.

The sea is a big deal in Mark and in the whole Bible and in mythology and in our psyches. It's amorphous, it's not solid, it's deep and dark. It's Tiamat's realm. It threatens our sense of security and order. The sea is what we don't know and can't control. Jesus sits on *that* and teaches from *there*. What a place to teach from. It doesn't seem like you'd get math blowing off that water. It seems like you might get something more unsettling and confounding.

The people are standing safely on solid ground, their feet planted firmly on what they know. Jesus sits on the surface of what is beyond them, out of their control, teaching in parables: shooting out tight little pellets of perplexity to knock them off their feet, to break up the ground they think is holding them. I think Jesus wants to confound our usual ways of understanding, wants to frustrate our usual attempts to grab on to things. He wants us to hear something that we can't process like we process other information, something that doesn't fit into any preconceived categories. I don't think it's because he's mean and wants to trick us. I think it's because what he wants us to know is something that language is inadequate for, something so vivacious that it can't be contained, something that overturns the way the world works. It's not something that can be explained, exactly. It's something that swells and bursts and transforms our hearts and souls and minds.

So Jesus talks about seeds and what happens to them. He says the seed is the Word, but he doesn't say what the Word is, whether it's one word or twenty or mercy or God or his teaching or the gospel. Mark doesn't really have very much actual teaching in his book compared to the other Gospels. There's no Sermon on the Mount, even. There aren't a lot of clear and straightforward messages. Jesus interacts with people in Mark and heals them, and he speaks in parables.

His words are not systematic and precise and simple and clear.

How is the Word (whatever unfixable, living, uncontainable thing that is) heard? Does the seed penetrate and get inside and take root? Does it get in and rearrange everything—your mind, heart, and soul, your way in the world? Or does it land on rock, solid ground, where birds can swoop in and pick it up and take it away and eat it? (And hey, good for the birds. Something about them does seem like they must eat it. Flying all around and singing and naked, not all dressing up in suits and driving machines and making weapons factories and dividing up the world between the good and the bad and making wars and trying to control the world.)

Does the seed get in just a little bit, even grow a little, but get choked by thorns, by "practical reality," the cares of the world, so that it has no life? How could it not get choked by practical reality? There are terrorists who want to kill us, bills to pay, criminals and sinners and corporations that are waiting to corrupt our children. The cares of the world seem enormous. We don't need the Word, we need lines to keep back the encroaching evil. And we need money. There are definitely thorns.

What does it mean that some of the seed lands on good soil? It's easy to read this parable and start thinking immediately about my soil. Do I have good enough soil to make the seed grow? Am I open to the Word? What's my soil like compared to other people's soil? And then I look at the parable as if it might provide me with some information about how to improve my soil. It seems like that should be the point, but maybe that's not really hearing. Maybe that's more like computing.

At the end of the passage Jesus says to the people, "Look at how you hear." The parable really doesn't provide instruction about how to be good soil. It's not giving them something to do; it's about hearing. It is about the ear. The ear is an orifice. Vision has to do with surfaces, outsides. Sound has to do with interiors. The ear is "the organ that produces the effect of proximity."[2] There is an outer, middle, and inner ear. Twisting, tunnel-like tubes, tiny bones, and microscopic hairs all play a part in hearing. Air molecules vibrate and move in waves into the orifice; the waves vibrate and bend the microscopic hairs, which send off nerve impulses that are then passed through the auditory nerve to the brain, which recognizes (or perhaps not) the sound. Though a lot of things are at work in hearing, we don't have that much conscious control over the process. Jesus asks the people to reflect on how they hear. He doesn't tell them eight ways to better our soil. Maybe because giving us eight ways to better our soil won't help us to hear, will actually keep us from hearing, will allow us to *grasp* when what we need is to *hear*.

It's frustrating that the Word is sometimes hard to understand, that you can't really put it through the machine, controlling the process. But maybe Jesus teaches in parables to confound us because what we need is to be confounded. Maybe because the whole way of being and thinking that we have learned from the cares of the world—the way that is part of the structure of our consciousness, that determines how we make our way through the world—needs to be transformed. We might like standing on rock. We may like being handed a brick more than having some breathing and baffling encounter that somehow undoes us, but in this parable *rock* is barrenness, something that can't give birth. Standing on the rock here is not hearing.

The language of parables does not build our confidence by building an argument we can follow. It's more of a language that calls attention "to the insufficiency of its own procedure."[3] Language can't capture this. Nothing can capture it. It isn't about capturing. It won't run through the normal machine. It breaks the machine.

The disciples ask Jesus about the verbal meaning of his teaching. They ask, "What do the words you said mean?" And somehow it seems like that is beside the point, or evidence that the seed isn't taking root, because you can't look at Jesus's words on the surface like that. The gospel in Mark isn't a specific set of teachings to be learned. It's more of a call to have the structures of your mind and your heart and your soul converted.

Maybe Jesus speaks in parables because he doesn't mean to give us answers or principles or something to be grasped. He means to induct us into a relationship. He's trying to get us to live in love with him, each other, God, the world. He's trying to get us to enter this struggle, which is not like having or knowing or grasping answers. It's like loving, which is not all that straight and not all that simple and not very reducible. Our "not understanding" might actually move us closer to life lived in relationship to the living God than eight steps to better soil could ever do.

Even though there may be a little bit of the trickster quality about Jesus here, there is also something serene about the way Jesus tells this parable, sitting calmly on the sea talking about a lot of seeds/words that don't get in and take root. Some do. And they grow big, sweet, and plentiful, "thirtyfold and sixtyfold and a hundredfold." There doesn't seem to be any question that there's going to be fruit, and a lot of it. And for all his frustrating opaqueness here, Jesus goes on to say that "there is nothing hid, except to be made manifest." The kingdom, it seems certain, will grow regardless of the state of our soil or the abundance of weeds or the ubiquity of rock. "It grows up and becomes the greatest of all shrubs, and puts forth large branches, so that the birds of the air can make nests in its shade" (Mark 4:32). Maybe right up next to the people who've finally come there to find rest.

12

How to Entangle Him in His Talk

Then the Pharisees went and took counsel how to entangle him in his talk. And they sent their disciples to him, along with the Herodians, saying, "Teacher, we know that you are true, and teach the way of God truthfully, and care for no man; for you do not regard the position of men. Tell us, then, what you think. Is it lawful to pay taxes to Caesar, or not?" But Jesus, aware of their malice, said, "Why put me to the test, you hypocrites? Show me the money for the tax." And they brought him a coin. And Jesus said to them, "Whose likeness and inscription is this?" They said, "Caesar's." Then he said to them, "Render therefore to Caesar the things that are Caesar's, and to God the things that are God's." When they heard it, they marveled; and they left him and went away.

Matthew 22:15–22

I think we should try to empathize with the Pharisees. It's maybe not that natural a thing to do, or that appealing, but

141

I think we should just try it. Say you're an actor and you have to be this character, get inside him. What might he be like? It would be a little too simplistic, too clichéd, to play him like the stereotypical villain. There's got to be a better reading. Pharisees are called snakes in the gospels, but of course they weren't really hissing, slithering creatures. They had legs and arms. They may have had really nice brown eyes, and even friendly voices. They weren't cold-blooded reptiles any more than we are, and if they had some sort of venom in them, it was probably a lot like the stuff that's running through our veins.

I don't know anything about acting, but I imagine there are techniques that might help a person get into a role, inhabit a character, find a way to get in touch with his or her venom. Don't be afraid to feel it, acknowledge it. Just go inside yourself for a moment. Close your eyes. Imagine that you're getting on an elevator on the top floor. Now push the button for the bottom floor and then take the elevator all the way down, deep down into your subconscious. Take it slowly, slowly. When you reach the bottom, the very bottom, get off. Okay, what do you see?

I know *venom* sounds so horrific and ugly, but honestly it's just a thing that helps a snake survive. I tried this earlier, and when I got off the elevator, I saw this venom, the pharisaical venom, and it wasn't all that foreign or unfamiliar. It was like self-justification, a scared feeling that makes one lash out in judgment or act with a certain superiority. Maybe not quite like adrenaline but semi-similar, like what starts pumping through your veins or brain cells when you feel threatened, some need to protect yourself. It didn't feel poisonous; it felt good, even comforting, like protection. Like self-protection.

The Pharisees were not actual vipers but, like us, humans. Think: people who are desperately trying to believe in God through their religion. They were guys who were trying to help other people believe in God. They were religious leaders. I'm not trying to say we should imagine the Dalai Lama, but I don't think we're getting at it very well if we always think of the blatant hypocrite.

The Pharisees were not friendly toward Jesus, but that's understandable. He wasn't really all that nice to them. The first time he sees them in Matthew he calls them "you brood of vipers." I mean, imagine that. You've been studying the scriptures all your life; you have a theology that makes sense to you, that helps you (and others) live. You have an idea who God is. Then this man shows up, this human. People are claiming he's the Son of God, people much less educated than you, and he calls you a *snake* and pretty much indicates that your beliefs and your image of God are all wrong. If I were a Pharisee, I could imagine having a hard time adjusting to this new development in the revelation. I could imagine having a hard time believing that God was actually behind it.

You don't have to think of them as super-villains to imagine why they might have had a hard time with Jesus, why they might have wanted to trap him. And what better way to do that than to entangle him in his own words, show that his logic is faulty or that his new take on things is all wrong or is completely impractical or won't really help anybody out. In the story in Matthew 22 that's what the Pharisees are trying to do, trap him in his own words. Snakes aren't so much bad in the Bible, they're smart.

Since Jesus began his ministry, he's been going around claiming that the Pharisees are wrong and unfaithful. But they don't think they are wrong and unfaithful. They think Jesus is. They don't think they lack faith in God. They think he does. And they want to show it. Can you imagine feeling something like that, if your way of life or your theology was threatened? I can. I think I probably do it all the time. And I doubt that if I were walking down the road in first-century Palestine and met Jesus I would immediately recognize him and embrace him and know that he is God.

In this passage the Pharisees come to Jesus with a question, supposedly. But they don't really have a question. They act like they are seeking instruction, but they aren't really. They aren't struggling with it in their souls. They aren't coming to him in pain or humility or need, with empty hands. They don't have a real question. It's more like they've been threatened, and they're ready to strike. They come up with a difficult puzzle that they think will stump him. They think they know both possible answers to their question, and they think either way he goes with it, he'll be trapped. They don't actually want dialogue—they want control.

Whether or not they are struggling with it in their souls, it is a good question, and important and smart. It's a huge question, whether to pay or not to pay taxes to Caesar. It's a question of how to live in the empire, that dominant oppressive reality all around all the time, constantly requiring you to submit to its rules, its music, its fashion, its food, its wars, its totality. According to the imperial reality, all the people fortunate enough to live in its domain owe their lives, their freedom, their allegiance to it. And you pledge your allegiance by paying taxes to the emperor. Should people who believe in God—the God of Israel, not Jupiter, not Caesar—pay this tribute to the empire? It was a big issue in the day.

The more revolutionary element of the Jewish people, the Zealots, said, "No way." If you believe in the sovereignty of Yahweh, you should not pay the tax. To pay the tax is to betray your God, your people. It's submitting to a system that crushes opposition, takes advantage of the poor and the humble. It's submitting to the monolithic lie. Don't do it. But if you take that stand, the empire will crush you, crucify you. And actually the Zealots did launch a rebellion, and they were utterly defeated and a lot of people were killed. If Jesus says, "Don't pay the tax," the Pharisees know he'll be arrested by the empire.

But if Jesus gives the other answer, if he says, "Yes, we should pay the tax," he's going to look like he's sold out his people. He's going to lose popularity and respect. The Zealots were heroes, champions, the resistance. If he says, "Pay the tax," it's going to look like he's accommodating to the loathsome tyranny. So what's Jesus going to do with this question? Is he going to dissent? Or is he going to be a good citizen of the empire?

I kind of know what way I would want him to go. But you know what? He doesn't go either way. It's actually kind of amazing what he does. It probably confounds both the rebels and the good citizens. Jesus doesn't say, "You should pay the tax," or "You should not pay the tax." He says, "Show me the money for the tax." You had to pay the tax specifically with Roman coins.

The Pharisees think, well okay, we'll go with that, and they reach into their pockets, fumble around a little, pull out a coin, and hand it to Jesus. Jesus points to the image on the coin and says, "Whose image is this?" Well, to say *image*, that's like saying *idol*. It's a pretty loaded word. You say *image* and lights start flashing and sirens go off for anyone who's familiar with the Hebrew scripture. They all know the polemic against idolatry. They know deep down in their soul that to bow down to idols, to serve them, is death. They certainly shouldn't be carrying any little idols around in their pockets. It's easy to miss the drama of this moment in the story, but in one quiet move, Jesus turns the whole thing around.

The Pharisees didn't come to Jesus with a real question. They weren't really very personally involved with the dilemma they posed. They just thought it was smart and tricky, and the perfect way of entangling Jesus in his own words. But actually they end up getting all entangled themselves. They've been walking around with the image of Caesar pressed up against their thighs. This gets them involved with the dilemma. They come all cool and smart and removed, and Jesus pierces their souls, practically draws blood. He makes it about them after all. He makes it concrete. Jesus plunges them into the struggle.

He shows them that you really can't live in the empire and not participate in it. They can't live in their world without participating in the economic situation. And they can't participate in the economic system without holding these coins. And they can't hold those coins without compromising what they believe in, their righteousness. It's like saying, "Sorry, guys, you can't remain pure. You can't stand back and judge. You can't justify yourselves. It's not possible. No one has clean hands."

You'd think Jesus might say, "Ha! *You* were trying to trap *me*? Who do you serve? Who's your master? You think you're faithful to God?" It's such a good opportunity to condemn them. But he doesn't do that here. He says, "Well, then, give to Caesar the things that are Caesar's, and give to God the things that are God's." I don't think he means to make a doctrine of the separation of church and state. I think he's speaking to the Pharisees in a way that will pierce them to the bone. It's not abstract, bloodless doctrine. It's Jesus, alive, encountering these living people.

There is something relaxed about the way he deals with this. He shows some confidence in something greater and bigger than Caesar. I think Jesus is showing the limits of the empire here. It's far from totality, however much it seeks to convince you that it is. Give to Caesar what is Caesar's. Give the empire its little coins. Give it back its idols, but of course you do not owe it your life. Life belongs to God. The Pharisees depart from this round in shock. They marvel. It undoes them. Be the Pharisee. What does it mean to give our lives to God? It's practically impenetrable. Of course we make it a matter of religion. We create rituals that help us as we seek to give our lives to God. We find answers that seem to solve problems for us, or the problems of the world, and we cling to them.

The Pharisees were not bad guys. It was their passionate belief that God was present outside of the temple, in the smallest details of life, that got them paying attention to the details. It was their recognition that God was at the dinner table of a peasant as much as in the temple that made them insist on the washing of hands and the saying of prayers. It wasn't about making elaborate rituals to keep people out. It was quite the opposite. They meant to cultivate a sense of God's presence wherever people walked and talked and breathed. God was not confined by the institution.

It was a "very important rabbinic insight . . . that God could not be described in a formula." [1] The whole point was to encourage a sense of the mystery and wonder of life, not to find neat solutions. "The Rabbis did not construct any formal doctrine about God. Instead, they experienced him as an almost tangible presence." [2] They believed deeply that their faith was expressed in acts of loving-kindness, especially to the poor and dispossessed.

They weren't actually rigid and inflexible. Luke Timothy Johnson says, "They were not tied to any particular social institution or political program. . . . They were mobile and adaptable. Above all, their perception of the people and

Torah was flexible and progressive and it was this that enabled them to represent the future of Judaism."[3] Their greatest genius was in their ability to read the texts and find continuing life in them. They believed that reading scripture was "a seeking out of God in our midst," not a rigid adherence to a static formula. The Pharisees invented midrash. I can hardly think of anyone I'd rather be. If I could be even just a little like a Pharisee, I feel like I'd be doing well.

Johnson describes a passage from the Babylonian Talmud that he says illustrates the spirit of the rabbinic tradition, what the Pharisees gave birth to, both in its "apparent frivolity and in its deeper seriousness." The passage discusses how many commandments God gave. One rabbi writes, "Six hundred and thirteen precepts were communicated to Moses, three hundred and sixty-five negative precepts, corresponding to the number of solar days, and two hundred and forty-eight positive commands corresponding to the number of the members of a man's body." More and more rabbis weigh in, until it is concluded that all the commandments may be summed up in this one: "Seek me and live."[4]

I am enthralled by what the pharisaical tradition has generated. I could only hope to ever read with a speck of the spirit of rabbinic inquiry. If we hear the gospel witness as warrant to point our finger at a particular group of bad guys, then it is not a text that has much creative potential to redeem.

We want life. The Pharisees wanted life. Franklin Graham says, "You can be alive in Christ tonight" in the Baltimore stadium, and thirteen hundred people walk the aisles because they want to be alive. It really isn't death and rock and rigidity that we're after, and yet somehow still we keep pressing the idols against our thighs. It's not the bad guys that wreck it all. None of our hands are clean. They are all speckled with plaster from the idols we build. Our knuckles are white from grasping so tightly. And Christ does not take the opportunity to condemn us. He says the word or does the deed that will set us free.

13

Tip the Boat Over

On that day, when evening had come, he said to them, "Let us go across to the other side." And leaving the crowd, they took him with them in the boat, just as he was. And other boats were with him. And a great storm of wind arose, and the waves beat into the boat, so that the boat was already filling. But he was in the stern, asleep on the cushion; and they woke him and said to him, "Teacher, do you not care if we perish?" And he awoke and rebuked the wind, and said to the sea, "Peace! Be still!" And the wind ceased, and there was a great calm. He said to them, "Why are you afraid? Have you no faith?" And they were filled with awe, and said to one another, "Who then is this, that even wind and sea obey him?"

Mark 4:35–41

The first part of the book of Mark has boats all over the place. Somebody gets into or out of one about nineteen times in the first eight chapters. In one verse "he immediately got into the boat," and two sentences later, he is "getting into the boat again." Jesus finds his disciples in a boat. When the crowds are getting too close, he gets into a boat. Boats are everywhere all the time.

This might not be all that remarkable if you live in the Bahamas or in the Land of Ten Thousand Lakes, but the story takes place in Israel, which has one lake, maybe two. For such a dryish setting, there are a lot of boats in Mark's story. It makes you think about boats. You could think for a long time. My husband has been making paintings of boats for twenty years. Some are cheerful and funny. Some are frightening in how they depict the precariousness of existence. Boats keep you floating on top of the water (the chaos, the uncontrolled, deep, dark abyss). They also put you at the mercy of the wind and the waves. You hardly need all the other words in the book of Mark; you could just say "boat" and be done with it.

I've been talking to my kids about the ocean lately, trying to get them up for a trip to the sea. Every time I do, Olivia starts whimpering and saying she's so scared and she doesn't want to go. I've been, honestly, mostly exasperated by what seems to me to be a sort of feigned drama (something she is good at both in a charming and occasionally irritating way), and I say, "Olivia, it's not scary. It's beautiful. You're going to love it," and Miles says, "Olivia, the sharks are way out. They never come close and you never see one," which I realize isn't entirely true. I've seen sharks.

Which got me thinking that maybe this whole thing Olivia was doing wasn't feigned drama after all, but archetypal fear. She asked me if there were going to be octopuses, and how big, and what about whales. Of course she's scared—she's imagining the deep, vast unknown. So I changed my tactic a little. I said, "You know, Olivia, it seems really scary until you get there, but once you're there it isn't that scary." Which I thought seemed profoundly true as a metaphor about our biggest fears, but then I almost immediately realized how profoundly untrue it could be.

The sea might be beautiful on a pleasant day on the shore, but what if there was a really bad storm? And what if you were in a boat on the sea in a big storm, and waves were rushing over the side of the boat, beating into the boat, and the boat was filling up with water, and what if Olivia was there? (It seems really scary until you get there, but when you're there it's not that scary? Right.) It's actually potentially one of the most horrifying things I can imagine. Are there people who would not be afraid? Boats promise you safety but lead you to death. I hate boats. I would like to be the person who was not afraid on a boat in a storm, but I would be afraid.

A bad storm blows up in the end of the fourth chapter of Mark. The wind and rain and beating waves are so loud the captain has to scream directions. People are tying themselves to lifelines. You know it's really bad because the disciples, who are experienced fishermen, think they are probably going to die in this one. And they're smart about this. Of course they are afraid. It is not at all hard to imagine that they would be afraid. What is hard to imagine is a guy lying there sleeping through it all.

It's almost impossible to imagine. In fact, about the only way I can imagine it is like a cartoon. Huge waves heaving the boat back and forth, and Pluto or Jughead or some thickish cartoon character with zzzzz's coming out of his mouth sliding all the way to the left. Sliding all the way to the right. Flipping, rolling, snoring. A huge wave crashes into his face. He opens one eye a crack, rubs his nose, and is back sleeping immediately. It's a stunt they pull in cartoons all the time.

153

There's someone sleeping, and somehow they fall out of a window or off the back of a truck or out of a tree and they stay sleeping. So I might be projecting, but there's something about the story in Mark that seems just a little funny to me. Not that Jesus looks dopey or thick, but you have to admit, it's a unique thing to do: sleep through a deathly storm while water's pouring over the sides of the boat.

The disciples behave more predictably in the situation: they panic. They maybe don't want to disturb Jesus, because he is their teacher whom they esteem and are a little subservient to, but I'm sure they are finally so exasperated that they think, "This is ridiculous. Wake up. Help us. Do you really not care if we die?" And they yell in his ear and shake him.

In the cartoon, this is where Jesus opens his eyes, one at a time, wipes the drool from his mouth with the back of his hand, shakes the sleep off, throws his shiny red cape back, charges up to the deck, raises his right arm and sends lightning bolts forth from it. He goes zip-pow-bam-pop, and suddenly the storm stops. And the unlikely superhero, free now from his drowsy stupor, back in his take-charge mode, says, "Why were you afraid? Have you no faith?" And all the disciples with little white sailor hats on their heads gather together and open their eyes wide and exclaim to one another, "Who then is this, that even wind and sea obey him?"

Jesus does not come across in the Gospels as simply an awesomely powerful hero. You may not see any comedy in the text, but one can hardly miss that the guy leaves room for questions. The disciples ask, "Who is he?" It's a big question (maybe an unending question, a question essential to our relationship with God), and if the disciples had stopped with that question, they might have shown how well they'd learned to be his disciples, how much they'd learned about what it's like to relate to the Other, how the Other eludes definition, resists frameworks. But they haven't learned that well yet. Who has? And they go on to make an assertion that betrays their desire for definition. It betrays what they want, what they're looking for. They want an answer, and this seems like a good one: he's the one that even the wind and sea obey. Who is he? He's a powerful miracle worker. That's a great answer, and it's probably satisfying to them to assert it.

But what about three minutes earlier when the great miracle worker was sleeping? What about when people are scared to death of dying, and may die, and they are bailing water and battening the sails, and he is sleeping? There's a way you can read this story where it seems like it's all resolved in the end. The disciples fear because they lack faith, and the whole story is resolved because in the end they meet the one whom the wind and sea obey. But really, in the end, is that who they meet?

Who is he? The whole story wraps around that question, and I don't think the answer is so simply or so singularly "the one whom the wind and sea obey," the one who can convince them to have faith or save them or love them or make everything right in the end by displaying the awesome power of God.

I don't think that's the answer, because I've read the rest of the story of Mark. It also doesn't make any existential sense to me. It doesn't seem true. I've never met a god like that. I don't have any experience of a god who makes everything right by awesome displays of power, a god who makes the storms go away. Every day boats go down. There are horrible storms in people's lives and hearts and minds, and people do go into the waves and drown. Is that because Jesus wasn't in their boat?

If they had Jesus in their boat, if you have Jesus in your boat (and you can wake him up), then you have nothing to worry about. Don't be afraid. He'll charge out of the stern, off the little cushion he's been sleeping on there, and bam-boom-pow, like Poseidon he'll make the storm go away and you'll be okay.

I don't even think the Greeks *really* believed in Poseidon. And I don't think that's what faith is. At all. Like, hey, you got Jesus in your boat? Better get Jesus in your boat, if you want a dry boat. I don't think the story resolves in this moment when the disciples look at each other and nudge each other and say, "See. Even the wind and sea obey him. Now we're getting it." Because in the end, whom do they really meet? What kind of god is this? The author raises the question, and I think it's the question we need to hold on to, not so much the clause that follows.

In the first half of Mark's Gospel, Jesus heals a lot of people and says to them, "Don't tell anyone." He keeps telling everyone to keep quiet about his power. Maybe because if they said anything, it would be all about how Jesus was powerful beyond all imagining. How he alleviated suffering, how he cured sickness and made everyone feel better. And though that might be a little true, it's not wholly true. It's not by awesome displays of power that God reconciles, saves, heals the world. Just read the end of the book of Mark.

In the first eight chapters of Mark, there are boats, boats, and more boats. Jesus sits in a boat, has a boat waiting for him, or walks on water to get to a boat. And then at the end of chapter 8, things turn. Jesus tells everyone he's going to suffer, be rejected, and die. After that, there's not one mention of boats again.

I think he tips the boat over.

He's not walking on the water anymore, he's not sitting in the boat; he's going in. He's taking the plunge. Suddenly, in the second half of Mark, it's not so much about miracles and power and magnificence. It's about suffering. Things shift from who is he?—even the wind and sea obey him, to who is he?—the Messiah who's going to die. Who is he, that these things could go together?

The disciples end up looking pretty bad in Mark, pretty dense. They never quite understand what Jesus is up to. It's not surprising. First he makes the sea obey him, then he drowns in it, sinks, displays no power at all at the most critical moment.

He's their leader, but look at him in the garden of Gethsemane the night before he's going to die. He sees it coming and he's afraid, just as they were during the storm. The tables turn: he asks *them* to stay awake. He goes and prays desperately that if it's possible he won't have to die, and when he comes back to his friends, he finds them sleeping. In the boat they asked him, "Do you not care if we perish?" In the garden, he asks them, "Could you not watch one hour?" He doesn't look like a mighty god. He looks vulnerable and sorrowful and needy. He looks a little like the disciples looked on the boat. But there's no bam-pow-bop now, no throwing the red cape back and raising his right arm. It goes from the disciples pleading, "Don't you care about us?" to Jesus on the cross crying out in not dissimilar fashion, "My God, my God, why hast thou forsaken me?"

In the beginning the crowds are always pressing on Jesus. The diseased want to touch him so they will be healed. And he wants the disciples to get him a boat ready. He wants a boat there to get into so that all the sick, clamoring, diseased crowds who are seeking healing won't crush him.

In the second part of Mark, he gives up the boat. No more boat. Now he's going to be with all the drowning sailors.

Maybe awesome power isn't the way to save the world. What do you need in a lover, in a relationship? Lightning bolts, or someone to know your soul—your fear, your need—and love it and never leave you alone? Never in any circumstance, any storm, any deepest darkest bottom. What's essential to love? Awesome displays of power, or a lover who does not despise your nakedness and shame and vulnerability? A god who calms the storm from a boat? Or a God who enters the depths for you?

Blood

14

Drinking to the Dregs

And he took bread, and when he had given thanks he broke it and gave it to them, saying, "This is my body which is given for you. Do this in remembrance of me." And likewise the cup after supper, saying, "This cup which is poured out for you is the new covenant in my blood."

Luke 22:19–20

The cup's passed around and one by one they tip it back, take a drink. It may be good wine; it may be cheap and crappy. It doesn't really matter. They take a drink. It affects their senses: they smell it, feel it on their lips, their tongues; they taste it, feel it go down their throats. It even hits their heads, depending, I guess, on how big a sip they take. Just literally drinking what the cup contains is a pretty full experience. The literal content of the cup is not lifeless or impotent, but the cup that Jesus passes around at the Last Supper, my God, what all's in there? It seems inadequate to say it's "heavily

161

symbolic." That sounds a little too stiff or academic to express what the cup means. To say *means* even seems a little flat or inaccurate. It's the Passion.

Jesus takes the cup after supper and says it is his blood. The wine may have been robust, but this intensifies the contents a little bit, don't you think? What does a sip of that taste like? How does that hit your head? He says the cup is his blood. That seems pregnant. That seems loaded. Though it doesn't seem exactly clear or concise to me.

The House of Mercy Band, our church band, occasionally plays in bars. They play bluegrass music and old hymns. Often they play "Nothing But the Blood of Jesus," which doesn't seem like something that would go over very well in bars, but for some reason I don't fully understand, it does. One night at the Turf Club, it was late and smoky and time to go, and I had just spilled a beer when the band broke into "Nothing but the Blood," and the whole place erupted into an ecstatic sort of frenzy, people dancing and singing and swinging each other around. Barflies, potheads, old heroin addicts, young music scene hipsters that have nothing to do with church, all blissfully, wistfully whipping about to "This is all my hope and peace, / Nothing but the blood of Jesus; / This is all my righteousness, / Nothing but the blood of Jesus. / Oh! Precious is the flow / That makes me white as snow; / No other fount I know, / Nothing but the blood of Jesus." I'm not exaggerating. It was very weird. And kind of beautiful.

I wouldn't have expected the crowd at the Turf Club to respond that vigorously to the blood of Jesus. Maybe it's some relic of primitive rituals, some barbaric gene from the past that got the people dancing. Or maybe it has something to do with the fact that for us, there is no life without blood. Maybe everybody was experiencing some sort of mass visceral response, some other-than-rational reaction to a song that makes blood hope.

"Blood is the fluid of life, transporting oxygen from the lungs to body tissue and carbon dioxide from body tissue to the lungs," says the Franklin Institute. "Blood is the fluid of growth, transporting nourishment from digestion and hormones from glands throughout the body. Blood is the fluid of health, transporting disease fighting substances to the tissue and waste to the kidneys. Because it contains living cells, blood is alive."[1]

In Chinese film and Japanese anime, a small flow of blood from the nose signifies sexual desire. Blood signifies intimacy. Kids (do they do this instinctively?) prick their fingers and mix their blood to show their love, fidelity, closeness. When Jim and I were deciding whom we should leave our children with if we die in a horrible plane crash or car wreck or bird flu pandemic, and we decided on our neighbors, our families protested. How could we leave them with someone who wasn't blood? But when Jim and I discussed that angle, I wanted it to be with my blood, he with his. Nothing runs deeper than blood, they say. For us, there is no life without blood.

But there is also a pretty significant aversion to blood in our societal consciousness. In some cultures, when a woman bled, she was sequestered to a tent or hut apart from the tribe.[2] Bleeding was shameful. Bleeding women were dangerous. Sir James Frazer writes, "An Australian [aborigine], who discovered that his wife had lain on his blanket at her menstrual period, killed her and died of terror himself within a fortnight."[3] Menstruating women were sometimes forbidden under pain of death to touch anything that a man used, or even to walk on a path that any man frequented. Blood is our life. It flows just beneath our skin, but it's also taboo.

In twentieth-century America, the aversion to blood often seems to be an aversion to graphic violence. But much graphic violence is fairly acceptable (a cartoon character pounded repeatedly over the head with a giant mallet, squished, and having his eyes burst out of his sockets on Saturday morning kids' TV) as long as there's no blood. Miles is playing RuneScape on the Internet, as are all his friends, even his friends who have super-responsible and careful parents, even his cousin whose mom is on top of everything media-related that might be inappropriate for growing boys. The characters kill each other, but they just sort of touch and vanish. There's no blood.

Sensitive parents don't tell their children stories about the giant hungering for the blood of an Englishman so much anymore. Or about Hansel and Gretel getting cooked by the witch. We change the stories a little bit, sanitize them. How did parents not recognize for all those centuries that blood-hungry giants and savage witches would traumatize the children? Stories where cute bunnies talk about love are more popular these days than the more traditional folktales where mothers died and people bled.

Blood may be intimacy and the fluid of life, but I am not happy or moved when I come into the bathroom in the middle of the night and find the remnants of Miles's having tried to deal with his bloody nose. Blood on the bathtub, blood in the sink, bloody Kleenexes strewn on the floor sticking to my feet when all I wanted was a quick drink of water and then to go back to sleep peacefully. Blood may be our life, but it's hard to deal with. I can see why we are uncomfortable with a God who comes and pours out his blood for many, with a fountain filled with blood. With a God who says, "This is my blood shed for you; drink it."

Jesus says the cup is his blood, and he passes it around for everyone to drink. It seems like it might be a little hard to hold on to that cup. What does it feel like in your hands? I would like to understand the contents of the cup. I think, if we could really see what it contains, we'd understand a lot. Or maybe *see* and *understand* aren't the right words. Maybe the right word is *taste*.

In the garden of Gethsemane Jesus prays that the cup might be removed from him. He may have simply meant, don't let me die. But it seems unlikely that Luke, Jesus, anyone would be just casually throwing around the word *cup* here (Luke uses the word *cup* once in the twenty-three other chapters of his book, and then four times in the space of twenty-five verses in the story of the Passion).

What's in the cup that Jesus gives the disciples? What's in the cup that he doesn't want to drink, but that he's going to drink? Not wine or grape juice or root beer. It's something dense and devastating and vital, somehow, to the salvation of the world.

It is thoroughly unsurprising, typically characteristic, that *cup* in our culture means something plastic. Cup has become so diminutive. It's like a mini or a lesser glass. It's plastic, or it may be paper. It comes in a dispenser. It has little jokes on it or Winnie the Pooh. It's the thing you give the kids to drink out of, or it's the thing you throw away. A Dixie cup. A kiddie cup. It's light. Church is one of the few places where *cup* seems solemn and heavy.

Wineglass evokes a very different response from *cup*. It doesn't have a lot of verbal weight, but I am readily aroused by the image: a wineglass two-thirds full of deep red wine. For months over the holidays, whenever I opened up my Internet homepage there was a perfect picture of a perfect glass of perfect red wine in the banner across the top. It was an advertisement for some silly holiday planning guide, but every time I saw it, it made me long for something. The image communicates a lot. Festive conversation, sumptuous meals, holiday cheer. I saw the nice wine in the nice glass and I felt like Pavlov's dogs. I instantly longed for whatever it contained.

The cups in the Passover meal that Jesus was having with his disciples had a little of that feel. They were symbols of joy. They were about freedom. Though early on in the Passover tradition the meal was to be eaten in haste, by the early first century the tradition had changed. To get ready for the Passover meal, you were supposed to lie back on a pillow and relax. And then as you sipped from the cup and ate the meal with ease (the ease was important), you were supposed to imagine, to regard yourself as if you personally had been freed from slavery in Egypt. The content of the cup was freedom, and you were supposed to drink it in and relax, feel the wonder of liberation, and sigh deeply with great pleasure.

The cup contains beautiful freedom. Gazing in it, we might be moved to festive celebration. But there is a grave side to the content as well. Actually, to say there is a *side* is misleading. Stuff doesn't sit in a cup on sides. It's the nature of the vessel to hold it all together, mixed up, inseparable. There are cups all over the Hebrew scripture. You should take a look at some of the cups in the Psalms and the prophets. There's some nice wine and some overflowing goodness and mercy. And there are some strange and wild liquids. Some of the cups make you drunk. It's as if the cups are full of some sort of magical potion, like a truth serum, that exposes you, strips you naked. Most of the time the stripping is communal: a nation is exposed. Sometimes it feels like the nakedness is just the precedent to being held and warmed. Sometimes it

seems a little cold and scary. Some cups you drink, drain-
ing the dregs, and then you pluck out your hair and tear
your breasts. The cups are full of anger and frustration and
separation and pain and love: passion.

Sometimes God is holding the cup and God is handing
it to a prophet and God says: You have to make all the nations drink this, "and if they refuse to accept the cup from
your hand to drink, then you shall say to them, 'Thus says
the LORD of hosts: You must drink!'" (Jeremiah 25:28).
Honestly, these cups, they seem about enough to make a
person vomit. They are deep cups, cups big enough to hold
about five bottles of wine, or even whiskey. And in fact, the
prophet says, "Drink, be drunk and vomit, fall and rise no
more" (v. 27).

One's cup often refers to the vessel that contains one's
lot, one's portion, but what is that? Your experience, what
happens to you, more or less your life: what you suffer, what
you love, what you feel and think. It seems like the cup is
the vessel, the place that holds it all. Everything.

I came across a place in Ezekiel where Ezekiel says to Jerusalem, the city of God: "You have gone the way of your
sister [Samaria, who makes love to the idols]." So he says,
Look, "I will give her cup into your hand . . . You shall
drink your sister's cup which is deep and large; you shall be
laughed at and held in derision, for it contains much; you
will be filled with drunkenness and sorrow. A cup of horror
and desolation, is the cup of your sister Samaria; you shall
drink it and drain it out" (23:31–34).

It got me thinking about my sister's cup, not my literal
sister, though it could be, or my brother, just all the people I
know and all the nations there are, and I thought how deep
and large the cups are, how much they contain. Unbelievably
dense and complex and sordid and beautiful and painful

histories. All the trauma and hilarity, fortune and misfortune; all the diamonds and water and salmon, and all the barrenness. All the destruction. There's all the love that people felt or didn't, and how all that interacts with their personal psychology, and their experience in the womb, and floods and famines and civil war and earthquakes. And I thought of how just about any of those cups, if I drank them, would fill me with drunkenness and sorrow and too much of everything, and I'm pretty sure I couldn't drink them to the dregs. My own cup is practically enough to make me fall down. Can you imagine drinking any more on top of that? It just about makes me nauseated to think of it. I can hear about other cups, but drink any other cup? I'm afraid I would vomit. I would vomit and fall down and rise no more.

It is said that St. Catherine of Siena, "when she felt revulsion from the wounds she was tending, . . . bitterly reproached herself. Sound hygiene was incompatible with charity, so she deliberately drank off a bowl of pus."[4] I can't imagine.

Jesus comes drinking, with an ease I can hardly even conceive, the cups of harlots and tax collectors, sinners, the lost, the greedy and needy and addicts and lepers, the unenlightened—dark, dense, deep, large cups that contain much. What a stomach he must have, what a tolerant constitution. I think the events of the Passion suggest that Jesus drinks his sisters' cups. And brothers' and aunts' and uncles' and cousins' and parents' and all the neighbors' and nations' everywhere, Samaria's and Israel's and Rome's. Drinks them all down to the dregs.

What alchemy transpires in his veins to create the elixir, the blood of life that has the power to cure all the ills of humanity?

There's a moment in the garden when Jesus doesn't want to drink the cup. But he does. The mercy drinks it all up, and it is dramatic. He drinks the hour of the power of darkness, and it kills him. Of course it does. That was in the mix. To say that the Passion is about Jesus suffering the wrath of God seems backward. What he suffers, it seems, is the life of the world.

God really gives Godself to the world in Jesus Christ, takes everything in and drinks it all down. And comes offering his cup for us to drink. I couldn't possibly drink my sister's cup. I'm not sure if I'm even willing or able to drink whatever it is that Jesus is pouring. What rich and wild blood it must be. What sort of nourishment does it transport, what sort of disease-fighting substances, what life?

Sometimes the church gets a little squeamish about Christ's blood. Maybe because the atonement has often been read in ways that seem barbaric or unhelpful. So we decide to focus more on Christ's life. But often it seems like trying to focus on Christ's life gets us doing the opposite. It gets us concentrating on ethics or a way of life, morality, teachings, something more bloodless, rational, and systematic than life. We don't have life without blood. Jesus says, "My blood shed for you," and whatever he meant by that does seem vital. However much the story has been distorted, I don't think it's crazy to keep looking to the blood of Jesus. I think maybe Jesus is giving it to us. And I hope that if we can't manage to raise it to our lips, Jesus might pour it down our throats.

15

Murdering God

Now at the feast he used to release for them one prisoner for whom they asked. And among the rebels in prison, who had committed murder in the insurrection, there was a man called Barabbas. And the crowd came up and began to ask Pilate to do as he was wont to do for them. And he answered them, "Do you want me to release for you the King of the Jews?" For he perceived that it was out of envy that the chief priests had delivered him up. But the chief priests stirred up the crowd to have him release for them Barabbas instead. And Pilate again said to them, "Then what shall I do with the man whom you call the King of the Jews?" And they cried out again, "Crucify him." And Pilate said to them, "Why, what evil has he done?" But they shouted all the more, "Crucify him." So Pilate, wishing to satisfy the crowd, released for them Barabbas; and having scourged Jesus, he delivered him to be crucified.

And the soldiers led him away inside the palace (that is, the praetorium); and they called together the whole battalion.

And they clothed him in a purple cloak, and plaiting a crown of thorns they put it on him. And they began to salute him, "Hail, King of the Jews!" And they struck his head with a reed, and spat upon him, and they knelt down in homage to him. And when they had mocked him, they stripped him of the purple cloak, and put his own clothes on him. And they led him out to crucify him.

And they compelled a passer-by, Simon of Cyrene, who was coming in from the country, the father of Alexander and Rufus, to carry his cross. And they brought him to the place called Golgotha (which means the place of a skull). And they offered him wine mingled with myrrh; but he did not take it. And they crucified him, and divided his garments among them, casting lots for them, to decide what each should take. And it was the third hour, when they crucified him. And the inscription of the charge against him read, "The King of the Jews." And with him they crucified two robbers, one on his right and one on his left. And those who passed by derided him, wagging their heads, and saying, "Aha! You who would destroy the temple and build it in three days, save yourself, and come down from the cross!" So also the chief priests mocked him to one another with the scribes, saying, "He saved others; he cannot save himself. Let the Christ, the King of Israel, come down now from the cross, that we may see and believe." Those who were crucified with him also reviled him.

And when the sixth hour had come, there was darkness over the whole land until the ninth hour. And at the ninth hour Jesus cried with a loud voice, "Elo-i, Elo-i, la'ma sabach-tha'ni?" which means, "My God, my God, why hast thou forsaken me?" And some of the bystanders hearing it said, "Behold, he is calling Elijah." And one ran and, filling a sponge full of vinegar, put it on a reed and gave it to him to drink, saying, "Wait, let us see whether Elijah will come to take him down." And Jesus uttered a loud cry, and breathed his last.

Mark 15:6–37

The story of the cross, the murder of Jesus, is a hard story to read. It's the climax of the gospel narrative. It's violent and graphic and sad, but it seems so strangely easy to glaze over, so hard to have any real feelings about. It might be because it's a moment in the text that we have handled so thoroughly by abstraction and proposition. It is narrative, but it's sometimes hard to read it that way. I hear atonement theory. I see thirty thousand Chick tract illustrations of the cross as a bridge (with men in suits and hats walking over it), the cross as a factor in an equation (the cross plus something equals something, or something plus something equals the cross, I don't remember). The church has considered it the pivotal moment, the center of everything, the key to it all. But our ideas about the way to read it are often so fixed that it's easy to get the sense that if ever there's a stone, it's here.

Phyllis Butcher, my junior-high Sunday-school teacher (I did, for real, have a Sunday-school teacher named Butcher, though her first name wasn't actually Phyllis), taught us that the story of the cross was a sort of transaction, more or less an economic one: something was owed and someone had to pay. God is righteous, sinless, and perfect and created the world to be this way as well, but we failed. We have sinned against God, and the wages of sin is death. God's beautiful righteousness can't tolerate unrighteousness.

It made sense: sin mars the perfection God intended. It's unacceptable. But God loves us and doesn't want us to have to pay for our sin, so God offered his son so that the son would pay the wage so that we wouldn't have to. The story of the cross is the story of paying the penalty. It allows God to forgive us our debt, because the debt's been paid. It satisfies the righteousness of God, and we get something for free. This, I think, is what Phyllis meant when she talked about grace. If we made some sort of rational decision to accept

173

the grace, we would go to heaven after we died. This, I'm pretty sure, was what Phyllis meant by eternal life. If we did not make this decision, we'd go to hell. I'm sure this version of the story didn't come from reading the account of the Passion in the Gospel of Mark, but it became increasingly difficult to read the story without that version hanging on every word.

I'm not sure what Phyllis wanted us to hear most from this—maybe that God loves us—but what my friends and I seemed to take away from it was that the way to gain security for ourselves was to give our allegiance to that transaction. It wasn't enough to give our allegiance to God; we must also believe that Jesus died for our sins. In exchange for our allegiance to this transaction, in exchange for our believing in this grace, Phyllis said, we would gain eternal security. That's what we actually called it: *eternal security*. I can see why people might be drawn to this.

What if you could get your children and all the people you love to do something that would guarantee them eternal security? All they had to do was make a decision. It seems like a compelling proposition. I can see why parents and pastors and grandparents would be drawn to this. I desperately want my children to be eternally secure from everything I'm afraid of: total chaos when our oil runs out and the resulting marauding bands of violent people with guns looking for food—avian flu, vacuous meaninglessness, tornadoes, plane crashes, bad marriages, war, propaganda, totalitarian machines, exclusion, and loneliness. I would like to guarantee that my daughter will never ride in a car with a boy who has been drinking, that my son will never ever have cancer.

I can see why people give their allegiance to this version of the story and want people they care about to do the same.

But it's laced with the promises of idolatry more than the uncertainty of faith. In this version of atonement, it isn't really relationship to the radically alive, unsystematizable, ungraspable, unfathomably merciful, Other lover who saves us, it is our decision to give our allegiance to a system that offers security. I learned from my evangelical upbringing that faith was all about our relationship with Jesus. And that's honestly (obviously, I guess) where I find hope, but I think that the terms of the relationship were often so prescribed and rehearsed and memorized that it didn't feel much like relationship was what I was being pointed to.

I know the church I grew up in was pulling threads from the same scripture I am using to try to understand the cross. And it doesn't seem very easy to weave them into a coherent whole. I certainly am incapable of it. But it seems to me that the threads have often been yanked and pulled and woven into something more calculable and anemic than the rich, red blood of Jesus. I don't know that I can talk about what transpired at the cross any better than Phyllis Butcher could, but I have some hope that whatever it is, it might free us to be naked with each other more than blame each other, confess more than condemn. And this probably has to happen every minute rather than once. I'm pretty sure it does for me, anyway. I go back and forth between confession and condemnation every thirty seconds or ten or two.

Whatever the murder of Jesus on the cross means or reveals, Mark thinks it is good news, something remarkably hopeful, which is a bit odd on the face of it. He begins the story of the good news with John the Baptist preparing the way of the Lord by calling everyone out to the wilderness, an unsettled place, away from their kitchens and fences and businesses, away from their normal domesticity, to be baptized. To die and rise. Mark says "all" the country of Judea and "all" the people of Jerusalem came out to the wild (1:4–5). It seems like a bit of an exaggeration, but still, imagine the scene—the city emptied out, farms abandoned, old people, moms, kids, youth group leaders, everybody in the wilderness waiting to be baptized. Mark practically could have stopped there, he's already suggested so much. But he's just getting started.

Mark immediately sets up a significant tension between the Son of God and what almost anybody might expect from God. Jesus makes his first appearance standing on the dusty banks of a muddy little river waiting with *all* the people to plunge in. He doesn't look very transcendent or holy or particularly righteous, even. The tension has immediate results in Mark's narrative. By the third chapter, religion is already plotting to destroy Jesus. The disciples, his followers, the founders of the church, always seem to be wanting or expecting a little something different from him. And in the end they betray and deny and abandon him. Religion, the crowds, the disciples, the world might want a god or a savior, but they don't seem to want Jesus.

This reaction isn't entirely surprising. If Jesus is leading people anywhere, he seems to suggest that it is to suffering and death, and other than that he doesn't have an entirely clear and unambiguous message to rally the people. Practically everything about him leaves a lot of room for questions. And maybe most people didn't have that much room. It seems like the same story we've heard over and over: people preferring the work of their hands or their minds or their religions, people preferring some image of God to God. But this is sort of the ultimate idolatry story. God comes into the world looking unabsolute, bearing dust from the desert, hardly transcendent, merely breathing and bleeding and eating and drinking, and the world kills God. God walks around among the people, right up close to them where they can smell God. They eat with Jesus, sit next to him at the dinner table, and probably even sleep next to him in a little room where they can hear him breathe, and they prefer their ideas, ideals, systems; the work of their own hands; their idols that don't "hear . . . smell . . . feel . . . walk . . . make a sound" (Psalm 115:4–8). God's living right up next to them, handing them bread and fish, and they never quite see it. They want something else, something different—bigger, maybe, or more obvious.

The religious authorities were trying to honor the God they believed in when they sentenced Jesus to death. The Romans were following the rules of their order, doing what it took to protect the peace. The crowds were looking for a revolutionary. None of it looks all that wrong. It all makes sense. Except that in trying to secure their god, or secure the world, or save themselves, they killed the savior.

Our idols seem so good and right and necessary to us. It seems like our lives and the life of the world depend upon them, like without them everything would be chaos and bad and anarchy and unbridled wantonness. It seems like without the structures we cling to, no one would know right from wrong or have any way to orient themselves in the world. Our idols seem like our lifelines; we feel like we might die without them. They provide a little more clarity than "Love God with all your heart and soul and mind and your neighbor as yourself" does. They offer something that is easier to grasp than a God who comes living and breathing and bleeding and says, "Follow me." Idols make a lot more sense than that, and they don't bleed, and they are much easier to follow because they are really the ways we've come up with all along, rather than the Other disrupting our ways. When the wholly alive and unfixable God comes, "leaving our powers of comprehension in disarray,"[1] it's no wonder we try to nail him to the cross.

The story of the cross in Mark reveals that whatever the ease or the sense or the apparent necessity of our idols, our clinging to the work of our hands leads, not to the peace and beauty and goodness we might have hoped, not to our salvation or the salvation of the world or the triumph of our best ideologies or eternal security, not to life—but to death, actually; murder, even, the murder of the God of life. Jesus comes healing and resurrecting, unparalyzing the paralyzed, feeding the hungry, making the deaf hear and the dumb speak. He comes to make alive. And the world, according to Mark, puts him to death. In Mark, it really doesn't look like Jesus dies because God demands death as a penalty for sin. It looks much more like the ways of the world lead to the death of the God of life. It doesn't look like God demands death in this story; it looks like the ways of the world demand it.

Idols may seem to give us life, but what could be any more destructive to our lives and the life of the world than putting to death the life-giver? Jesus comes loving scandalously, without regard for rules or boundaries; feeding with abandon, making more than enough bread in the desert to satisfy crowds. He forgives unrestrainedly, offensively. And the world puts to death this most gracious lover. What could be more homicidal, more suicidal, than murdering unconditional love?

The story may seem like simply a hopeless condemnation of the ways of the world. But Mark thinks it's the good news. He's been fairly determined about that from the beginning. Maybe because it reveals the end of our gods, and it also reveals the heart of the Other. And maybe that revelation is the beginning of a stunning and hopeful freedom. Maybe it's somehow the way to peace and love and redemption.

Making love

Phyllis Butcher believed in a god whose righteousness could not tolerate unrighteousness. Righteousness meant for her, more or less, being "good" according to the culturally prescribed definitions that surrounded her, a sort of tangled mixture of advertising campaigns and what she learned from Bible Baptist Church. "Good" included a lot, everything from owning the right kitchen appliances to having a just and pure heart. It meant staying thin and wearing the right clothes. Her god had a pretty profound effect on her life. She believed in the cross of Christ's redeeming love, but still. Knowing that the god who can't tolerate unrighteousness was in the background, knowing that he was the absolute that was over and under and all around everything, made her live in fear of everything that was intolerable according to her culturally prescribed definitions of good, everything that might be intolerable:

1. In herself
   the bulge in her waistline
   her left profile
   her "ugly angry face," as the kids called it
   anger
   untoward feelings
   feelings
   needy weakness

2. In everything that surrounded her
   the bulge in her son's waistline

unattractive people
angry faces
anger
untoward feelings
feelings
needy weakness
hippies, liberals, Muslims, Jews, Hindus, drug addicts.

If she yelled at the kids, she hated herself for three days. If she or—God forbid—someone else saw in her motives or actions something inside her that was not "good," it sent her into paroxysms of defense and self-hatred and elaborate mechanisms of denial. It kept her from really knowing herself or being herself because she was too afraid to look at who she was or be who she was. Although she claimed to love people and believed she loved people, she was quite good at identifying what about her friends and neighbors was intolerable. And there were whole categories of people who lived almost entirely in that space. Her god may have ordered her world and helped her know right from wrong, but he didn't really free her to live in unguarded love.

Ludwig Feuerbach said, "By his God thou knowest the man. . . . Whatever is God to a man, that is his heart and soul." His (or her) religion is "the revelation of his [or her] intimate thoughts."[2] What we call God is really the projection of our own qualities, our ideas, onto a deity, fixing them, objectifying them, and then worshiping what we have made. Feuerbach thought that by projecting what is really ours onto God, we fail to live up to our creative potential. Mark seems to suggest it might make us murderers.

For all their apparent usefulness and sensibility, the story of the cross reveals the dark side of our idols. We can't really trust the gods we make. They may seem to help us,

180

but they might also destroy us, or get us destroying others. They aren't even alive, they can't love or move or forgive. They don't have hearts. Worshiping them isn't life-giving, it's death-dealing. The Psalmist is adamant about the dark side. He says that in serving their idols, people poured out "innocent blood" (Psalm 106:36–38).

The righteousness that can't tolerate unrighteousness is something I know quite intimately. I live on a gravel road in rural Minnesota. About a mile from our farm, there is a fairly new split-level house with light blue aluminum siding. Recently a lot of people from the city have bought three or four acres of what used to be family farms and put up similar houses in the middle of what used to be cornfields. They look misplaced and ugly to me. I look at them and I see the dissolution of the family farm and the encroachment of the suburbs and pretty much everything that's wrong with the United States. I dislike them. I particularly dislike the light blue house. Heavy drapes are always drawn over the windows. The inhabitants have not made any gestures towards embracing the land. Every time I pass the house, I wonder why the people never pull their drapes open, plant a flower, or come outside. I assume they are watching TV, some right-wing propaganda or *Extreme Makeover*. I have never met these neighbors, but I am fairly convinced that they don't share my values.

The other day when I was running past the blue house, loving the countryside where I can run without dodging vehicles or breathing exhaust, I saw and heard and smelled the man from the blue house perched on his red Lawn-Boy tractor, smoking and making his way to his mailbox. His mailbox is about twenty feet from his front door. I felt a sense of loathing. I tried to give a little bit of a wave, rise above my unfriendliness, but he seemed too focused on his cigarette and his mailbox to notice me. My heart started to beat faster, and my pulse quickened, and I felt some surging sort of breathless, vaguely exciting rage. I ran faster, eager to share my disdain with Jim.

I burst in ranting to Jim that he would not believe the most recent transgression unfolding at the blue house. Not only does the guy sit inside all day in the dark watching TV and supporting Bush, he actually drives his enormously toxin-emitting, stinky, loud, global-warming-creating machine twenty feet to get his mail. He seems to lack a moral center, a regard for beauty. He seems pretty clearly deaf, dumb, and blind. I suggested we find some way to destroy his Lawn-Boy. It wasn't just riding the lawn mower to the mailbox. I've been offended for months at the size of his lawn. It's pointlessly huge. I have never seen anyone playing croquet or volleyball or picnicking or walking or standing or sitting or setting one foot on his enormous lawn. Apparently the only time he comes out of his house at all is to wreak destruction on the environment. I began to enjoy my umbrage. I made Jim laugh. I could hardly wait to deliver the rant to all my good neighbors, my friends who share my disdain for the growing suburbanization of the rural landscape.

There's something satisfying about righteous anger. I felt a lot of clarity about my position. Something about the righteousness that can't tolerate unrighteousness seems really good and true and, I think, often even makes one feel alive, burning with rage against injustice or stupidity or evil. But what if God came and revealed Godself as not that god? What if instead of backing up our absolutes, God unraveled our idolatry, revealing that our allegiance to our gods is not really the thing that will make us or the world good, but something that leads to death?

The righteousness that can't tolerate unrighteousness is very familiar. It seems to be a prevalent trait of humanity. It's run-of-the-mill. It's normal. It's the way humans behave across the spectrum—mercenary capitalists, the coalition to impeach George Bush, fundamentalist Christians, Unitarians. It might even be what's necessary to make institutions run smoothly. It might be good business practice, but it's not grace. And however right and good and normal it seems, it's a stance that leads repeatedly to death. Pro-life advocates kill people, people in service to Islamic ideals kill people, people in service to Christian ideals kill people, people in service to revolution kill people, people in service to democratic values kill people—lots of people, children by the droves, and not only kill, but torture and mock. It seems that we get security from our allegiance to our idols, that we must protect the good, our absolute, that it's necessary if there's going to be any semblance of order—but it leads to death.

In Mark's story of the Passion, Jesus is mocked and tortured, dies a long, drawn-out, torturous death at the hands of people who are serving their ideals, their idols, their good. Everyone in the story turns out to be against him: the fundamentalists, the liberals, the revolutionaries, the collaborators. And he is against no one. The Son of God here looks nothing like the god who can't tolerate unrighteousness, the god who must put to death what is against God. He takes what is against him. He takes it all over his body. Lets it rip his flesh, expose his vital organs, strip him naked, pierce him to his heart. It makes him bleed. He suffers it all, and it kills him.

He doesn't look like a martyr, someone trying to protect "good." If that is what he's doing, he doesn't do a very good job of making it clear what the cause is. He doesn't make any clear statements before his accusers, "Give me liberty or give me death," "For God and country," "Viva la revolución." Not even "For the people!" Maybe because he's so inexpressibly, unsystematizably for everyone and everything, for all of creation that's been groaning in travail waiting to be set free from its bondage.

The Son of God on the cross looks nothing like anything anyone thought of as god or as savior. Jesus didn't look righteous or mighty or transcendent. If this was the Son of God, then it was like God was emptied out and refilled with things they barely recognized as God, with things that had little relation to God in their usual vocabulary. Jesus certainly doesn't look like a god who smites the unrighteous, who demands death; he looks like a god who dies. You'd expect God to act in a way that might get people to bow down. Jesus doesn't act much like he's trying to get anyone to bow down to him.

He's not a very good idol. He's anti-idol; he looks weak and quiet and vulnerable and unformidable, not good and right and clear and strong. He doesn't seem to be about looking like a good thing that we would want to give our lives to. Instead, he gives his life to us. And to what possible end?

The prophets were always trying and trying and trying to get the people to understand that God doesn't want sacrifices: God wants relationship. God doesn't want burnt offerings: God wants intimate knowledge. Maybe the pivotal moment, the center of everything, isn't about God's demand for a sacrifice, but the revelation of God's relentless pursuit of communion. Maybe God gives up looking righteous and holy and transcendent and strong, maybe God chooses vulnerability, because God's not looking to be our idol, a good we bow down to. God's looking for love, and this is the way to love. And God's looking for life. Not life at the expense of life, but big and spacious and fecund life, life that is thick and complicated and full of all sorts of things, contradictions; not pure and simple and straight, but vivacious and creative and inclusive.

Maybe the unrighteousness God can't tolerate is separation, not-love, and the cross isn't about paying a wage, making an economic transaction. It's not keeping a deal. It's making love. Making communion. It doesn't look much like God wants people's relationship to God to be like their relationship to their idols. God doesn't want to be a god to whom we give burnt offerings, an ideal we would kill for. God wants to be our lover and to make us lovers. Perhaps the center of everything is the way to that.

Jeremiah was a prophet who suffered, writhed, displayed the agony of God because, he says, God's people don't know God. And by *know* he didn't mean to have rational apprehension of an abstract or objective concept. By *know* he meant something thoroughly intimate, more like sex than objective certainty. They didn't know God, according to Jeremiah, because they'd become obsessed with the work of their own hands. They cut down a tree and deck it with silver and gold and fasten it with hammers and nails so that it cannot move, and then they worship it. He says their idols are but "scarecrows in a cucumber field" (Jeremiah 10:3–5), and the people are prisoners to them.

Because of this, the covenant ("I will be your God, and you shall be my people," Jeremiah 7:23) is severed. Rather severely. They are not God's people any longer. They have given their lives to their idols. It seems like the end of the story. But then Jeremiah starts talking about a new covenant that God will make with the people. God's not going to give up on them. God's going to abolish their unrighteousness, their lack of connection, their lack of intimate knowledge by writing it "upon their hearts" (Jeremiah 31:33). Ezekiel expresses the same thing this way: God says, "I will take out of your flesh the heart of stone and give you a heart of flesh" (Ezekiel 36:26).

There's something vaguely appealing about the sound of a heart of stone. It's solid and invulnerable, maybe unmoving, but strong and not easily broken. A heart of flesh sounds more fragile, vulnerable, more subject to injury and pain.

It is usually said that the new covenant in Jesus' blood has something to do with the conversion of hearts. Maybe the conversion is not so much to a way, but to flesh.

Stone may be strong and clear and clean and absolute and stable, but it's not alive. Maybe God is trying to make our hearts fully alive, and maybe that involves breaking them open. The conversion we need is nothing like bowing down to an idol. It's like seeing all the idols, everything we're used to clinging to, crashing down. All the systems of protection and defense—everything we've ever clung to to keep us separate from the unrighteous, the bad, the weak, the wrong, "or the sick or the fat or the tired or the drunk or the mean or the dumb or the ugly,"[3] the man in the blue house or the people in the red states or suicide bombers—come crashing down.

Christ does not die on the cross in subservience to a God that demands death, he dies in order to defeat death, in order to reveal our addiction to death and idolatry so that we might see and be freed from our subservience. The story of the cross is the story of the subversion of our gods. Alison says that with the death of Jesus, "the murderous lie is exposed in its entirety."[4] It is a breathtaking freedom. We discover that God is not the righteousness that can't tolerate unrighteousness, but love. Alison writes:

Here we have the element of the discovery of the absolutely vivacious and effervescent nature of God leading to

186

the realization that behind the death of Jesus there was no violent God, but a loving God who was planning a way to get us out of our violent and sinful life. Not a human sacrifice to God, but God's sacrifice to humans. . . . The phrase "God is love" is not one more slogan which we can tack on to the end of other things we know about God and which we can brandish when we feel like it. It is the end result of a process of human discovery which constitutes a slow and complete subversion from within of any other perception of God. That God is love is a certainty achieved in the degree to which it came to be discovered that God has nothing to do with human violence and death, and as it became clear that God has so little to do with those things that he was capable of subverting them through Jesus being expelled as a sinner to show that the goodness and justice of God have nothing to do with our fatal and expulsive notions of goodness and justice.[5]

We may be reluctant to let go of what has provided us with some sense of fragile security. But what if instead of making gods, we could live trusting in the love of the God who saves the world through grace? Really. Not just a concept you accept, but an incomprehensibly marvelous, inconceivably inclusive, profligate love that could overturn the world as we know it. It's hard to believe it's safe to give up idolatry for love, to give up god-making for this unmanageable, foolish communion, but it seems like something that would change the world.

Maybe God is working on dissolving the stone. Maybe having our hearts turned to flesh—being made alive—makes us see more and hear more and be more awake than could possibly be comfortable. But maybe our discomfort is God calling us into a different way of being, one that no longer clings to our systems, our absolutes. Maybe God is calling us into relationship. Not just some sort of bond between ourselves and our friends, but something that stretches us out beyond our limits, beyond the limits of what we have previously known, beyond ourselves and our gods. And it's not very neat, and *easy* isn't a good word for it. Burnt offerings are easier. Distance is less painful. Law is much less messy. Subservience is safer. But Jesus comes to set us free.

16

Everlasting Life

On the sabbath they rested according to the commandment. But on the first day of the week, at early dawn, they went to the tomb, taking the spices which they had prepared. And they found the stone rolled away from the tomb, but when they went in they did not find the body. While they were perplexed about this, behold, two men stood by them in dazzling apparel; and as they were frightened and bowed their faces to the ground, the men said to them, "Why do you seek the living among the dead? Remember how he told you, while he was still in Galilee, that the Son of man must be delivered into the hands of sinful men, and be crucified, and on the third day rise." And they remembered his words, and returning from the tomb they told all this to the eleven and to all the rest. Now it was Mary Magdalene and Joanna and Mary the mother of James and the other women with them who told this to the apostles; but these words seemed to them an idle tale, and they did not believe them.

Luke 23:56–24:11

Most days I wake up in the morning feeling like I know what to expect. Toast with peanut butter, probably some sort of cantankerous morning conflict between the children, Jim's reaction to the conflict, Jim's reaction to my reaction to the conflict, a commute where I will feel aggravated by someone who insists on driving two feet from my bumper, and some good things too, of course. It is so easy to believe there is nothing new that we don't really even look for it. We have files for everything, and we trust our files. There are types of people, types of experience, types of shows and music and clothes. We can hardly encounter someone or something without filing it. It is how we've learned to understand.

It's like your brain (I think this might even be scientific) gets ruts in it, develops pathways. And your parents and teachers and preachers seem to actually urge you to make the ruts. Look. When you drop a glass, it breaks and creates a mess. It isn't an amazing experience of sound and light reflecting off hundreds of shards of diamondlike glass. It's a *mess*. I have to clean it. The man in the donut shop who cleans the floors and offers complex illustrations of how what's outside his skin is no different from what's inside his skin, of how he melts into his broom and his broom into him, is *schizophrenic*. If you don't want what the church tells you you should want, you're *wrong*. And pretty soon the ruts are so defined that the neuroelectric impulses (I might be making this up a little) can hardly travel anywhere else but those well-worn pathways. The ruts get too deep for anything to jump out, and so everything just starts slipping into the ruts. Experiences, encounters, sights, sounds, people—all categorized and filed, and you're rarely aware of anything new.

It's a survival mechanism, the rutted brain. It helps me operate efficiently, get food on the table, plan for the future.

We learn to make fewer messes, live safely, conform to society or pictures in magazines. It's how we've learned to get along in the world, but it dulls us. It confines our imagination. It may give us a foundation, but it limits our capacity for love and transformation, variation and vitality. It makes monotony where there needn't be, cogs where there might otherwise be butterflies. Possibility is shoved and cramped into some narrow little space. And we're less alive. The tomb seems like the ultimate rut. It defines impossibility. And we believe in its definition. Death is the absolute absolute, and we live subservient to it, the prince of the power of the air. We breathe it in and it clogs our lungs, breathe it out and pollute the world with its corrosive power. Jesus dies. The prince defeats him. It must have been devastating to anyone who was following him, hoping he was the deliverer sent by God. He is put in a tomb. It is surely disappointing, but on the other hand everyone knows how to behave. Death isn't unusual at all, and so they do what they know how to do. They follow the old order. They prepare the spices, prepare the ointments. Careful not to violate the Sabbath, they rest according to the commandment. There might not be astonishing new hope in the order, but there is some sort of security in it, or at least there is piety and propriety.

In the morning they head to the tomb, and they find the stone rolled away.

Not vaporized, but rolled to the side. The ultimate container is opened. The women go to the tomb knowing what they are doing, knowing what to expect, thinking they are acting perfectly properly, and they are met with a challenge from two men in gleaming apparel, dazzling like lightning. The men say, "Why do you look for the living among the dead?" This is alarming, like a huge siren going off: the truth is not what you think, what you're used to, what you expect.

Just try to categorize this, file this. Where? The neuroelectric impulses are jumping out of the ruts like crazy. There's no place for this. Your usual apparatus for knowing? It doesn't work.

The prince's throne room is empty. The men standing by in their bright costumes (perhaps sequins, rhinestones, pink feathers) ask, "Why do you seek the living among the dead?" It's a big question. It's a creatively powerful question. It's a thoroughly judging and redeeming question. Why do we make bloodless belief systems our gods, give our lives and our energy in subservience to death? Why do we look for the living, look for life, security, ground, righteousness, happiness, cues for how to walk and talk and act and be—why do we ever look for this among the dead, try to get this from what has no life? Why do we ever long for fifteen minutes of hollow fame from the vacant media, an artificial innocence derived by imagining an evil other, a cheap sense of belonging to this or that over against them and those? Why would we keep looking to form our identities by grasping at concepts and images and fixations that have no life? Why would we keep worshiping idols?

I have been thinking a lot about some fish I saw recently at the Great Lakes Aquarium in Duluth. There were these big trout and walleye and I don't know what all in huge three-story tanks, and you could sit right up next to the glass and get really close to them. So I put Olivia on my lap, and we sat there for a long time. I know this may seem like I'm weird or like I was high, but I wanted to really see them, understand them, get them—fish: this other life form. So we watched and looked in their eyes. And they were blank. Blank eyes. Blank everything. Fish just swimming around in circles all cloudy-eyed, bumping up against each other and the glass, so unconscious, so unaware of anything.

You could put a quarter in a machine and get food to throw to them. Not like writhing, jumping live minnows, but little pellets of cat food mixed with ground-up fish. Dead food. And the walleyes and trout would swarm and dart for it and fight each other for it like it was precious, like their life depended on it. What life? It seemed so weird to me that you could even call this "life." They seemed hardly alive at all. They seemed like half-dead, unseeing, utterly unconscious creatures, completely lacking vitality. I tried to get Olivia to think they were cool, but all I could think was, "I have never had so much motivation for increasing my level of consciousness, of enlightenment, so that if there is some remote chance of reincarnation I will not come back as a fish."

I went on and on talking all the way back to the hotel about the fish and their dead eyes and wondering if you could rightly even call them alive, and maybe they used to have independent bookstores and they used to eat fresh spinach and beets from the garden, but then Wal-Mart and Barnes and Noble and Monsanto smothered every trace of generative irregularity out of their existence, and now they are hopeless and dismal and deadish. But then Jim, who likes fish a lot, and who often thinks beyond the moment a little better than I do, gently suggested that I remember the salmon we watched in the Northwest. How they leapt with libidinous fervor up the river, and how I nearly cried because they were so beautiful and hopeful. He said, of course the fish seem different when you are watching them swim round and round in tanks. They swim in circles and eat cat food pellets, not because they are hopeless creatures, but because they are in an aquarium. Imprisoned, they are living an unnatural half-life, all these utterly false limits imposed on them. They aren't hopeless creatures; they just need to be let loose. I wanted to go back and free the fish. And I got the kids into shouting and chanting, but of course we didn't. We would have been arrested, and the walleyes had probably eaten so much manufactured food that they couldn't survive in the wild anyway.

When the stone is rolled away and the tomb is shown to be empty, the king of idols is exposed as "no more than a frightening mirage." This has the potential to turn the world upside down, free the fish, un-rut our brains. James Alison says, "In the light of the resurrection we can look back and see how up to then the whole pattern of living had been cast in terms of death and its associated fears."[1] The apparently absolute absolute is shown not to be definitive and powerful after all. What seemed forever fixed is unfixed. The captives are set free.

The resurrection doesn't cancel death out, as if it were a real king with real powers that must be overcome by violence, but rather "the whole mechanism by which death retains people in its thrall had been shown to be unnecessary. Whatever death is, it is not something which has to structure every human life from within (as in fact it does), but rather it is an empty shell, a bark without a bite."[2] The resurrection frees us to be unconfined by fear, to quit seeking fake security. "There are almost an infinite number of ways of seeking fake security. Typically but mistakenly, we regard this grasping as intrinsic to being human ('it's human nature'), rather than as a sad distortion of that being."[3] The resurrection enables us—practically forces us—to revise our perceptual categories, our estimations of what is real, again and again, to question all of our files. Not out of shame, but out of some growing sense of the uncontainability of God's love.

Paul says, "For as in Adam all die, so also in Christ shall all be made alive" (1 Corinthians 15:22). What is it like to be made alive? We die a little somehow in our process of human culture-making. We build strip mall after repetitive strip mall, make wars, do violence, like there was no choice. We hate and arrange and label, and things just keep falling into the ruts, the files. And we trust our files. It's ingrained in our brains that good is limited. And we live in anxious rivalry for that limited good, limited love, dully and unconsciously bumping up against each other, all filmy-eyed and unseeing, swimming in circles, occasionally getting up to fight each other for fake food.

What is it like to be made alive? To have our brains unrutted, to have our imaginations transformed, to slowly and surely realize that there is no limit, none at all, to the love of God? The good is not limited. It is out of our control—it is being grown in old tires, in the corners of donut shops, in the cracks in the cement, in little boxes on people's back porches, in unkempt and irregular places by an exuberant lover of the vastest array of fruit.

17

Reverse Glory

When Jesus had spoken these words, he lifted up his eyes to heaven and said, "Father, the hour has come; glorify thy Son that the Son may glorify thee, since thou hast given him power over all flesh, to give eternal life to all whom thou hast given him. And this is eternal life, that they know thee the only true God, and Jesus Christ whom thou hast sent. I glorified thee on earth, having accomplished the work which thou gavest me to do; and now, Father, glorify thou me in thy own presence with the glory which I had with thee before the world was made.

"I have manifested thy name to the men whom thou gavest me out of the world; thine they were, and thou gavest them to me, and they have kept thy word. Now they know that everything that thou hast given me is from thee; for I have given them the words which thou gavest me, and they have received them and know in truth that I came from thee; and they have believed that thou didst send me. I am praying for them; I am not praying for the world but for those whom

197

thou hast given me, for they are thine; all mine are thine, and thine are mine, and I am glorified in them. And now I am no more in the world, but they are in the world, and I am coming to thee. Holy Father, keep them in thy name, which thou hast given me, that they may be one, even as we are one. While I was with them, I kept them in thy name, which thou hast given me; I have guarded them, and none of them is lost but the son of perdition, that the scripture might be fulfilled. But now I am coming to thee; and these things I speak in the world, that they may have my joy fulfilled in themselves. I have given them thy word; and the world has hated them because they are not of the world, even as I am not of the world. I do not pray that thou shouldst take them out of the world, but that thou shouldst keep them from the evil one. They are not of the world, even as I am not of the world. Sanctify them in the truth; thy word is truth. As thou didst send me into the world, so I have sent them into the world. And for their sake I consecrate myself, that they also may be consecrated in truth.

"I do not pray for these only, but also for those who believe in me through their word, that they may all be one; even as thou, Father, art in me, and I in thee, that they also may be in us, so that the world may believe that thou hast sent me. The glory which thou hast given me I have given to them, that they may be one even as we are one, I in them and thou in me, that they may become perfectly one, so that the world may know that thou hast sent me and hast loved them even as thou hast loved me. Father, I desire that they also, whom thou hast given me, may be with me where I am, to behold my glory which thou hast given me in thy love for me before the foundation of the world. O righteous Father, the world has not known thee, but I have known thee; and these know that thou hast sent me. I made known to them thy name, and I will make it known, that the love with which thou hast loved me may be in them, and I in them."

John 17:1–26

I heard an interview on NPR with a guy who wrote some book about a Buddhist interpretation of history. I really wasn't listening very well. But the thing I heard that struck me, and that I can't quit thinking about, was his claim that our sense of what history is has changed dramatically in the last few centuries. History used to be more just all sorts of people recording all sorts of things they thought were worth remembering. Like what day the trees blossomed or the river rose, or the night the neighbors came over and everyone drank wine and danced and someone made up an odd song that you wouldn't want to forget. History was more just the wild and prolific and unruly mix of uncommon and ordinary lives lived.

But in the last two hundred years or so, our sense of history has been almost entirely focused on important figures, the powerful, the glorious, the people who make a name for themselves. History is conceived of as the thing these people make. The prolific and unruly mix of wild and ordinary lives lived is not very significant in comparison. People say this or that was a historical event, like every other event isn't. Our sense of what history is has dramatically narrowed.

This sense of history is obviously a perception that has a lot of power to shape the world. We've been trained to focus our attention on a very narrow strip of people and events, and we believe that this narrow strip determines the world, is history, is what carries significance and meaning. Some people try like mad to gain access to the strip, to become powerful or famous. Others watch it and live vicariously.

What if that conception of history was subverted? What if everybody started to become convinced that meaning and power and significance weren't really in the narrow strip, quit focusing on the powerful, and noticed the thirty thousand other prolific and interesting things that go on around us all the time? It seems like it would change everything. Somehow, it seems like there would be fewer McDonald's and chain stores and magazines with Brad Pitt on the cover. Maybe every grocery store would have different magazines in their racks, like homemade magazines by old ladies and people who lived next door, and maybe people would talk more to their neighbors if we believed what was going on in our neighborhood was history as much as what's going on in the White House, if talking to some guy on the street weighed as much as talking to Terry Gross, if it was apparent that an Iraqi or American soldier equaled George Bush, if there weren't some people who were more important than others, if what we considered historically significant was different, if we started noticing a jillion things we're not used to noticing: how a bug moves in the grass or a bird eats. It seems like everything would be different.

Right before Jesus prays for his disciples, he says, "I have overcome the world." What he means by that, I think, is that he's undone the misconceptions that shape the world, he's unraveled the story the world tells. He has made history *his* story. Sorry to make such a cheap, easy, old evangelical-tract-like play on words, but somehow it seems like it works. Because his story is such a wildly different story, a story where the sense of what is significant has been completely turned around. It deconstructs the conventional sense of power and the conventional social world's order—what the world has come to depend on. It seems dangerous to the world because it disregards its order. His story brings eternal life, he says, unlimited life. It opens up completely different possibilities, unconfined, not at all narrow.

Jesus prays this prayer right before he's going to die. He's praying, "Glorify me." I always balk at that, because I'm thinking in terms of the usual story. It sounds like a pretty

200

conventional prayer, something Andy Warhol might have sent up to the press. It can seem like Jesus wanting his story to be such a big deal is exactly the same as everyone else who wants to be a big deal. Like he wants to make history, just like Alexander the Great or Bob Dylan. It seems like he might be saying that he thinks he should be famous. It sounds like what he wants is for the world to admire him. But the very odd, astounding, unheard-of thing is that *glory* for him has nothing to do with people admiring him. He knows his moment of glory is going to be dying on the cross, being rejected in every way by religion, government, friends, and every single angle of the social consensus. Seeking approval is pretty much the opposite of what he's doing.

He's not seeking glory from the old glory machine that's fueled by anxious grasping after fake security, fear of death, some self-seeking need for attention. He is not praying to be counted as significant in the social order. He's not asking God to help him navigate the machine. He isn't worried about the machine. He simply doesn't believe in it. His story isn't about him trying to make space for himself, a name for himself. It's about opening up history in a way that will make room for everyone. His isn't the kind of glory that's about some One being great; it's about all being one.

That's so entirely different from the old machine. Jesus dying on the cross and rising from the dead is not Jesus taking his place at the top of the same old order. It deconstructs that whole project, deconstructs the old glory machine, sucks out all the old content of glory and power and death and replaces it with something very different, very spacious, and very relaxed. His glory is the grace of God.

He's not defining a new line that we must cross to access power or to be among the good or the great or the righteous. He's not instituting the ultimate game of us versus them. He is undoing the lines. The lines lose their meaning. The desire to be righteous, transcendent, or "better than" loses its meaning. Power loses its meaning. Death loses its meaning. Jesus' approach to glory might get people shaking off the haze of the old definitions and wondering, "Why do we quarrel, try to outshine each other and keep grudges against each other?"[1] Why have we been so enthralled and subservient to death? But it won't be the same machine in different colors, or with nose rings or tattoos.

If God becomes the one the social order rejects, the one everyone is over against, the one on the bottom—if God dies—it's like jamming a log into the gears of the old machine. It breaks it. If God has taken the place on the bottom, what can it mean to be on top? Nothing. Jesus' death exposes the uselessness and utter futility and violence and exclusiveness and meanness of the old glory machine, of deriving our value, significance, or serenity over against anyone else's. Ever.

Jesus doesn't make a new machine for shooting different sorts of people to the top. He sits in the place of the one on the bottom, the one everyone is against, though not in shame or some sort of false humility, not to wallow in feelings of being bad and nothing and dirt and useless. It is his *glory* to sit in this place.

His glory "doesn't displace us but makes us alive."[2] It reveals something remarkable about the love of God. Something very different from—in fact, the opposite of—idolatry. Something that might be called *reverse glory*. It is so different from how we're used to thinking about how to be good, and what is required to order the world, and power and honor and glory, that it is a little hard to conceive of.

He is praying that his disciples will somehow manifest this glory as well, that they will be held in this truth, that they will follow him. It is a very weird calling. Believing in his story instead of history might make people appear a little odd. In Jesus' culture (and ours too), glory and honor were all about public recognition. So to claim some sort of glory or honor that is not publicly recognized hardly even makes sense. It doesn't fit the definition. It seems foolish. Whoever would say such a thing obviously doesn't get it, practically doesn't even understand language, much less the social order. But Jesus refuses to get it from the old machine, and his refusal redefines, deconstructs, and overcomes the world.

Jesus prays that his disciples—the church, whoever has glimpsed the unraveling—will keep it going, remember it, cherish his glory that overcomes the world. He prays that the world's ways will keep unraveling. That his followers will keep remembering not to find a home in the world, but rather in the utterly spacious love of God. He prays that whoever has glimpsed real glory will go ahead and look crazy and weird and like they don't get it, because they won't get it from the old machine. He prays that if we ever find ourselves rooting around in the gears of the old machine (for me it's probably thirty thousand times a day), we'll remember we're free. We'll remember that the old machine doesn't even work. God jammed a log in it. It's broken. There is eternal life. There is a more beautiful and true and merciful glory where all are one. And it isn't boring or rigid or exacting or priggish or prudish or puritanical or artificial; it's where joy may be fulfilled. It is perhaps a little bit hard to define how to be a follower of that, but it is what Jesus prays.

The boy in the crosswalk

I was picking the kids up the other day after school, and I watched this adolescent boy walking across the crosswalk. He was the kind of adolescent who seems like he might not fare too well in the eyes of the social order in terms of complexion, clothes, hair, eyes, shoes, body, style, the way he moved. And I was thinking as I was watching him, because I've been having this horrible insomnia, "God, I would rather be him than go one more night without sleep." It was a sort of rash prayer. Which sent me into a sort of extended consideration of what it would be like to be him. And I thought, man, we need the conventional social order to unravel. If all this kid gets is the machine? If he's going to learn his value, significance, through conventional culture? He won't stand much of a chance. Of course, I don't know him. He may be incredibly funny or smart or some other thing that the world values. He might get through puberty and become a different creature. But there are very many people who do not have much that the world values. There are a lot of people whom conventional culture can hardly tolerate, whom the machine tramples and spits out. I felt so clearly, so painfully, that if there's not something other than conventional culture to help form us, a lot of us are in trouble.

But there is something else. I know there is. I have confidence there is. How else would any of us survive? We can't live at the mercy of the world, because the world does not have enough mercy to go around. We don't get our life from our idols; they don't have any to give. We live by the grace of God. Maybe if you get enough props from the machine, you don't think it needs to deconstruct. Maybe you hold on to it or at least think its staying in place wouldn't be so bad. But, you know, the world needs it to deconstruct. And it *has* deconstructed. Collapsed. Don't hold on to it anymore. You don't live by it. You live by the grace of God.

A couple of nights after my rash prayer that didn't work, we took the kids to the Royal Rangers' archery shoot in the elementary-school gym. The kids had brought home flyers from school that said, "Learn archery from experts with real bows," and both of them really wanted to learn archery with real bows. So we took them, even though neither Jim nor I wanted to. And I have to confess I was totally creeped out once we got there. Because it was all a fundamentalist Christian thing sponsored by the local Assemblies of God, and they had flyers urging kids to accept Jesus and inviting them to summer camps where they would provide youth with camping, devotions, Bible study, crafts, sports, hiking, and friendships. And the Royal Rangers were all dressed up in army-like uniforms, and I thought it was evil, and they had tried to trick us into coming, and they were bad.

I wanted to define myself over against them, and actually did quite a bit of that sitting on the floor next to Jim. We laughed and whispered at the offensiveness of the army theme and the gall of their bait-and-switch tactics and the insensitivity of their obviously narrow definition of Christianity.

And then I saw that boy, the adolescent from the crosswalk. He looked kind of better in his Royal Ranger uniform, and he was helping little kids position arrows on their bows. And I thought, I bet the Royal Rangers have helped him to define himself by the love of God instead of the conventional social consensus. I bet they have provided him with devotion and Bible study and friendships and freedom from the machine. And I felt like I trusted God. If the something other can come through in the Royal Rangers, I can trust that it's coming through all the time, all over.

We're all in this together in a profoundly thorough way. Free in moments and also side by side on the assembly line. The idols I crank out tend to have some sort of feminine colors and maybe a stripe of some weird antirational thing going on, mixed in an unlikely manner with shades of Barth and lefty polka dots. The Royal Rangers' idols are definitely of a different sort. I don't know how we make ourselves let go of our idols. I doubt if we can or do. But I believe that from time to time we might hear a clink, some little echo signaling to us that they are hollow. I don't think these are moments of despair as much as moments where we glimpse that what holds us is the grace of God.

FOOD

18

Delight in the Fatness and Live

Now when Jesus heard this, he withdrew from there in a boat to a lonely place apart. But when the crowds heard it, they followed him on foot from the towns. As he went ashore he saw a great throng; and he had compassion on them, and healed their sick. When it was evening, the disciples came to him and said, "This is a lonely place, and the day is now over; send the crowds away to go into the villages and buy food for themselves." Jesus said, "They need not go away; you give them something to eat." They said to him, "We have only five loaves here and two fish." And he said, "Bring them here to me." Then he ordered the crowds to sit down on the grass; and taking the five loaves and the two fish he looked up to heaven, and blessed, and broke and gave the loaves to the disciples, and the disciples gave them to the crowds. And they all ate and were satisfied. And they took up twelve baskets full of the broken pieces left over. And those who ate were about five thousand men, besides women and children.

Matthew 14:13–21

Ho, every one who thirsts, come to the waters; and he who
has no money, come, buy and eat! Come, buy wine and milk
without money and without price. Why do you spend your
money for that which is not bread, and your labor for that
which does not satisfy? Hearken diligently to me, and eat
what is good, and delight yourselves in fatness. Incline your
ear, and come to me; hear, that your soul may live.

Isaiah 55:1–3

I love the idea of people being miraculously fed, magical
feasts, bread multiplying outrageously to feed everyone. I
like stories where food is miraculously manifested. When
my kids ask me to tell them a story, I almost compulsively
end up there. They are probably so sick of it. It's not like
I even mean to go there, but I end up there anyway. Some
kid is on an adventure or maybe lost and hungry and she
ends up somewhere—in another world or a hollow tree—
and then, out of nowhere, there's food floating around or
set out beautifully on a table or hanging on trees. And it's
usually like nothing she's seen or tasted ever before, super-
juicy and delicious and satisfying. Or some kid's lost in the
woods, starving and hopeless, and he gets fed by chipmunks
and butterflies. Or you eat or drink some sort of magic thing
that transforms or transports or frees you.

It's not just me. That sort of thing is all over folktales and
fairy tales—enchanted beans, the pot that never empties,
magic banquets. I think it has to do with some primal hope
or desire that there is enough somehow, somewhere. However
outrageously or unbelievably, somehow there is enough that
hunger might actually be satisfied. It seems unlikely. But I
love a story where Dumbledore, with a twitch of his wand,
makes a dusty bottle of the finest honey-colored mead and
four glasses appear, or chicken legs and pomegranates and
large chocolate cakes.

There are some great feeding stories in the Bible, really good and wild and miraculous ones. It's like the narrative will be going along fairly sensibly and then *pow!*—suddenly some sort of unrestrained and unreasonable fatness emerges.

Like the manna in the wilderness. The people have escaped from slavery in Egypt. They're free. But then they're walking around in the wilderness and they're hungry and they start thinking, "Why didn't we just stay in Egypt where we sat by the pots of meat?"

If I were the God who had just freed them, I think I would say, "Fine. Then go back and sit by your old pots of meat in Egypt." But instead, God actually says. "Okay. You're hungry? I will rain bread from heaven." And the people find this mysterious and miraculous bread all over the ground every morning. And in the evening quails come up and cover the camp so the people get their meat (Exodus 16).

There's another story where this woman's husband dies and she has no money. Nothing. And the creditors are coming to take her children away, and Elisha says, "What can I do to help you? Tell me anything you have in your house."

She says, "I have nothing. Nothing."

He says, "C'mon, tell me one thing."

She says, "I have one jar of oil."

So he says, "Okay, go out and get all the empty vessels you can find—pans, bottles, buckets, old plastic containers, anything you can find in your neighbors' yards or beside the road. Get as many as you can. Then go into your house and shut the door. Then pour the oil from the jar into the containers." And the widow keeps pouring and pouring, and the oil fills up everything, all the empty vessels.

And Elisha says, "Now go and sell the oil and pay your debts." And the widow and her children are able to live on that unexplainable, crazy abundance for the rest of their lives. That's in the Bible (2 Kings 4:1–7).

I really love this one: there's this huge, horrible famine and drought going on, and God tells Elijah, "Just go out and live in the wilderness." And so he goes out there with nothing, and he's probably thinking he's going to starve to death, and maybe he doesn't care. He sets up camp and goes to sleep, and he wakes up in the morning to see these ravens flying into his camp with bread and meat hanging from their beaks. And they just drop it off for him. And in the evening, the ravens fly back in with more bread and meat. And he drinks from a brook (1 Kings 17:1–7). I want to camp by a brook and be fed by ravens.

Then there's the story of the feeding of the five thousand, which seems to be pretty major since it appears six times in the New Testament in slightly different versions. In the Matthew 14 version, Jesus takes a boat out to a lonely place, but as it turns out, there are tons of people waiting for him when he gets there. Which might have been sort of a drag, but Jesus adjusts to it. Jesus has compassion on them. And they all hang around and hang around. And it gets late, past suppertime. And the disciples finally say, "Look, we should probably send all these people away now to go buy food for themselves in town."

But Jesus says, "They don't need to go away. Feed them."

They say, "Well, we don't really have any food to give them." But Jesus takes the little they come up with and blesses it, and all the people are fed. More than five thousand, from five little loaves and two little fish. And everyone is filled and satisfied, and there are basketfuls of bread left over.

People often say there's a moral to this story: Share. You feed them. I tend to make my stories to my kids have a moral point. "Share" is a good one. "Don't be greedy" is another good one. And certainly in folktales and fairytales, there's almost always a moral. But the miraculous feedings in the Bible aren't like that. It's more like they are these little breaks in the middle of a fairly sensible narrative, where suddenly there's an absurd and irrational and mysterious abundance. Where things have been barren or lacking or hollow, where there has been need, suddenly there is miraculously prolific food—bread raining from heaven, birds flying in to deliver meat and bread.

In Isaiah, God says, "Delight in the fatness and live." That sounds like the opposite of "Despair in the emptiness and die."

"Ho, every one who thirsts, come to the waters; and he who has no money, come buy and eat!" The voice in these narratives really doesn't have the tone of "Try harder to be better," or "Quit complaining and go out and get food for yourselves," or "Make sure what you're carrying in your pocket is worth something." It's more like "Relax. Don't be anxious. Delight in the fatness and live." It's not the voice of shame or scarcity or reprimand. It's not even the voice of reason. It's more like the voice of a lover wooing the beloved.

The gospel is less a demand that we manufacture the good than an invitation to live gratefully and generously, radically embraced and embracing. I think that hearing "Don't be greedy, and share your toys, and be good" does something different to us from hearing "Incline your ear and come to me, so that you may live."

When Jesus says to the disciples, "No, they don't have to go out and buy food. You feed them," he isn't telling them to go home and bake bread. He's not demanding that they come up with something. He's confident that it's already there. Jesus doesn't demand feeding in this story. He breeds it. Miraculous feeding stories don't create the sort of climate or mood that setting up an accounting table might, where everybody has to stand in line and show what they have. They create the mood of a party, where there's just an enormous abundance of unbelievable food provided and wine all around, and it's obviously never going to run out, and you're eating and drinking and enjoying it, and if somebody walks up and they look a little lost or hungry, of course you're like, "Hey, have a glass of this wine." And you start handing them wine and you're like, "You've got to try this cheese with it. And taste these strawberries, man, they're good."

Miraculous feedings are about something that isn't scarce. At all. They aren't about oil, obviously, or the world's resources or our money or our altruism or our righteousness or our willingness or our anything. They are about something infinitely abundant, something outside of us that relates to us and to the world in a way that will transform everything. They show us a glimpse of a place where we can believe there is no scarcity, where we can believe in infinite abundance; so of course we're inviting everyone in and handing out plates of cake. And we're not at all afraid someone's going to take our plate or our place or get there first.

Even though Jesus says in this story, "Hey, nobody has to go out and buy the food," it seems like we still are constantly hearing "You've got to go and buy the food." And I just don't think hearing that breeds feeding. It gets us more in this place where we're like, "Okay, I know I've got to buy the food, and it's hard, and I don't have enough money, and I'm tired and totally overburdened, but I know I have to do this thing that is right." And then we look over at our neighbor or George Bush or some guy smoking on his tractor or some group that seems to be distorting the gospel of Jesus Christ, and we've been sweating and trying like a dog to do what's right while they just seem to be wrecking everything or controlling the world with money and power. We're working so hard to buy the food, and we look over and those people don't seem to be working at all, or what they are working on seems bad. And it breeds not-love. And we sure as hell aren't going to invite those bastards over for a glass of wine on our back porch or offer them any cake.

But what if we didn't hear "You've got to buy the food"? What if we heard instead the ravens' wings flapping as they flew in with meat and bread in the morning and meat and bread in the evening? As William Stringfellow says, "The characteristic of the life of God which the church needs most to recall nowadays . . . is how absurdly simple [God's] action in the world already makes our witness to [God] in the world." [1] He writes,

> The Christian faith is not about some god who is an abstract presence somewhere else, but about the living presence of God here and now, in this world, in *exactly* this world, as [people] know it and touch it and smell it and live and work in it. . . . The meaning of Jesus Christ is that the Word of God is addressed to [people], to *all* [people], in the very events and relationships, any and every one of them, which constitute our existence in this world. That is the theology of the Incarnation. [2]

Delight in the fatness, and live.

Notes

Chapter 1: Nooses and Knots

1. Eduard Thurneysen, *Dostoevsky*, trans. Keith R. Crim (Richmond: John Knox, 1964), 72.

2. Huston Smith, *The Religions of Man* (New York: New American Library, 1958), 134, 136.

3. Karl Barth, *Church Dogmatics*, vol. 2, part 1, trans. G. W. Bromiley (New York: Charles Scribner's Sons, 1956), 159.

4. Thurneysen, *Dostoevsky*, 54.

5. Bruce Benson, *Graven Ideologies: Nietzsche, Derrida and Marion on Modern Idolatry* (Downers Grove, IL: InterVarsity Press, 2002), 190. Emphasis in the original.

6. Friedrich Nietzsche, *Twilight of the Idols*, in *The Portable Nietzsche*, trans. Walter Kaufmann (New York: Viking Penguin, 1982), 479.

7. Jean-Luc Marion, *The Idol and Distance*, trans. Thomas A. Carlson (New York: Fordham University Press, 2001), 6–7.

8. Marion's word, from Benson, *Graven Ideologies*, 192.

9. Ibid., 11.

10. Mircea Eliade, *The Sacred and the Profane: The Nature of Religion*, trans. W. R. Trask (New York: Harper Torchbooks, 1961), 79.

11. Ibid., 22.

12. Benson, *Graven Ideologies*, 19.

13. Ibid., 224.

14. Ibid., 198.

15. Ibid., 197.

16. Ibid., 186.

17. Ibid., 119.

18. Ibid., 203.

19. Ibid., 141, 143.

20. Nora Ephron and Susan Edmiston, Bob Dylan interview, in *Bob Dylan: A Retrospective*, ed. Craig McGregor (New York: William Morrow, 1972), 84.

21. Ibid., 86.

22. Nat Hentoff, "Bob Dylan, The Playboy Interview," in *Bob Dylan: A Retrospective*, 136.

23. Karl Barth, *Church Dogmatics*, vol. 2, part 1, 274.

24. Karl Barth, *Church Dogmatics*, vol. 1, part 2 (Edinburgh: T & T Clark, 1978), 431.

25. Fyodor Dostoyevsky, *The Brothers Karamazov*, trans. Constance Garnett (New York: New American Library, 1957), 62.

26. Benson, *Graven Ideologies*, 196.

27. James Alison, *Undergoing Good* (New York: Continuum, 2006), 18.

28. Marion, *The Idol and Distance*, 198.

29. Benson, *Graven Ideologies*, 196.

30. Ibid., 207.

31. James Alison, *Raising Abel* (New York: Crossroad, 2003), 38.

Chapter 2: Ancient Riddles

1. Frederick Buechner, *Wishful Thinking* (New York: Harper and Row, 1973), 8.

2. William Placher, *Narratives of a Vulnerable God* (Louisville: Westminster John Knox, 1994), 110.

3. Ibid., 92.

4. Ibid., 88.

5. James Alison, lectures at House of Mercy Church, May 2005.

6. Karl Barth, *The Word of God and the Word of Man* (New York: Harper and Brothers, 1957), 32.

7. Donald Bloesch, *Essentials of Evangelical Theology*, vol. 1 (San Francisco: Harper and Row, 1978), 53.

8. Karl Barth, *Church Dogmatics*, vol. 1, part 2 (Edinburgh: T&T Clark, 1978), 719.

9. Ibid., 719.

10. Bloesch, *Essentials of Evangelical Theology*, 77.

11. Susan Handelman, *Slayers of Moses* (Albany: State University of New York Press, 1982), note 30.

12. Ibid., xiv.

13. Ibid., xvi.

14. Avivah Gottlieb Zornberg, *The Particulars of Rapture: Reflections on Exodus* (New York: Doubleday Image, 2001), 4–5.

15. Ibid., 5.

16. Jean-Luc Marion, *The Idol and Distance*, trans. Thomas A. Carlson (New York: Fordham University Press, 2001), xxxvii.

17. Handelman, *Slayers of Moses*, xvii.

18. Ibid., 116.

19. Zornberg, *The Particulars of Rapture*, 2.

20. Handelman, *Slayers of Moses*, 17.

21. Zornberg, *The Particulars of Rapture*, 5.

22. Handelman, *Slayers of Moses*, 56.

23. Zornberg, *The Particulars of Rapture*, 6.

24. Stephen Moore, *Mark and Luke in Poststructuralist Perspectives: Jesus Begins to Write* (New Haven: Yale University Press, 1992), 150.

25. Handelman, *Slayers of Moses*, 71.

26. Ibid., 94.

27. Moore, *Mark and Luke*, 150.

28. Friedrich Nietzsche, *Twilight of the Idols*, in *The Portable Nietzsche*, trans. Walter Kaufmann (New York: Viking Penguin, 1982), 480.

29. Zornberg, *The Particulars of Rapture*, 13.

30. Avivah Gottlieb Zornberg, *The Beginning of Desire: Reflections on Genesis* (New York: Doubleday, 1995), 64.

31. Handelman, *Slayers of Moses*, 79.

32. Ibid., 56.

Chapter 3: In the Beginning

1. Avivah Gottlieb Zornberg, *The Beginning of Desire: Reflections on Genesis* (New York: Doubleday, 1995), 14.

2. Ibid., 18.

Chapter 4: The Original Lie

1. James Alison, lectures at House of Mercy Church, May 2005.

2. Robert Thurman and Tad Wise, *Circling the Sacred Mountain: A Spiritual Adventure Through the Himalayas* (New York: Bantam, 1999), 110.

3. Alison, lectures, May 2005.

4. Phyllis Trible, *God and the Rhetoric of Sexuality* (Philadelphia: Fortress, 1978), 111.

5. Karl Barth, *Church Dogmatics*, vol. 4, part 1 (Edinburgh: T&T Clark, 1978), 422.

6. Ibid.

7. James Alison, *The Joy of Being Wrong* (New York: Crossroad, 1998), 243.

8. Ibid., 261.

Chapter 5: A Midrash on the Tower of Babel

1. Bruce Benson, *Graven Ideologies: Nietzsche, Derrida and Marion on Modern Idolatry* (Downers Grove, IL: InterVarsity Press, 2002), 204.

2. Avivah Gottlieb Zornberg, *The Beginning of Desire: Reflections on Genesis* (New York: Doubleday, 1995), 59.

3. Ibid., 58.

4. Ibid., 63.

5. Ibid., 61.

6. James Alison, *The Joy of Being Wrong* (New York: Crossroad, 1998), 167.

Chapter 6: God's Mouth on Our Nostrils

1. Wikipedia, s.v. "life," http://en.wikipedia.org/wiki/life (accessed May 10, 2006).

2. Avivah Gottlieb Zornberg, *The Beginning of Desire: Reflections on Genesis* (New York: Doubleday, 1995), 61.

3. John Seabrook, *Nobrow: The Culture of Marketing and the Marketing of Culture* (New York: Random House, 2001), 220.

4. Ibid., 109.

5. See Deuteronomy 30:15–20; Psalm 106; Isaiah 44–48; Jeremiah 10–12; Ezekiel 14.

6. Carl G. Howie, *The Layman's Bible Commentary: Ezekiel and Daniel* (Atlanta: John Knox, 1977), 17.

Chapter 7: Two Mule-Loads of Dirt

1. I owe much of this reading to Jacques Ellul, *The Politics of God and the Politics of Man* (Grand Rapids: Eerdmans, 1973) 23–40.

2. Ibid., 39.

Chapter 8: The Ultimate Anti-Idolatry Story

1. Susan Handelman, *Slayers of Moses* (Albany: State University of New York Press, 1982), 82.

2. Karl Barth, *Church Dogmatics*, vol. 4, part 2, trans. G. W. Bromiley (New York: Charles Scribner's Sons, 1956), 497.

3. Karl Barth, *Witness to the Word* (Grand Rapids: Eerdmans, 1986), 89.

4. Ibid.

5. Karl Barth, *Church Dogmatics*, vol. 1, part 2 (Edinburgh: T & T Clark, 1978), 720.

Chapter 9: The Mother of God

1. Abingdon Press, *The New Interpreter's Bible*, vol. 9, Luke–John (Nashville: Abingdon Press, 1995), 521.

Chapter 10: A Pathological Attraction to Revolutionaries

1. *The Works of Philo Judaeus*, trans. Charles Duke Yonge (London: H. G. Bohn, 1993), http://www.earlychristianwritings.com/yonge/book29.html (accessed June 5, 2007).

2. Rabbi Aryeh Kaplan, *Sabbath-Day of Eternity*, a publication in the Joseph Tanenbaum Library Series, http://www.ou.org/publications/kaplan/shabbat/39.htm (accessed July 5, 2007).

Chapter 11: Look at How You Hear

1. Stanley Fish, *Self-Consuming Artifacts* (Los Angeles: University of California Press, 1972), 378.

2. Jacques Derrida, *Margins of Philosophy*, trans. Alan Bass (Chicago: University of Chicago Press, 1982), xviii.

3. Fish, *Self-Consuming Artifacts*, 378.

Chapter 12: How to Entangle Him in His Talk

1. Karen Armstrong, *The History of God* (New York: Ballantine, 1993), 74.

2. Ibid., 73.

3. Luke Timothy Johnson, *The Writings of the New Testament: An Interpretation* (Philadelphia: Fortress, 1986), 53.

4. Ibid., 56–57.

Chapter 14: Drinking to the Dregs

1. The Franklin Institute: Resources For Science Learning, s.v. "Life-blood," http://www.fi.edu/biosci/blood/blood.html.
2. Rev. Scott Swanson, a pastor from Vancouver, BC, brought this up when I was giving a workshop at St. Andrew's Wesley Church.
3. Sir James George Frazer, *The Golden Bough* (New York: Macmillan, 1922), http://www.bartleby.com/196/40.html (accessed June 8, 2007).
4. Mary Douglas, *Purity and Danger: An Analysis of Concepts of Pollution and Taboo* (Harmondsworth, UK: Penguin, 1966), 17.

Chapter 15: Murdering God

1. Bruce Benson, *Graven Ideologies: Nietzsche, Derrida and Marion on Modern Idolatry* (Downers Grove, IL: InterVarsity Press, 2002), 230.
2. Ludwig Feuerbach, *Essence of Christianity*, trans. George Eliot (New York: C. Blanchard, 1855), 33, http://books.google.com/books?id=Lsvo-mgtueOc8dg=the+essence+christianity+by+ludwig+feuerbach (accessed June 8, 2007).
3. Paraphrased from lyrics of a song written by my friend Brett Larson.
4. James Alison, *Raising Abel* (New York: Crossroad, 2003), 24.
5. Ibid., 46, 48.

Chapter 16: Everlasting Life

1. James Alison, "Violence Undone: James Alison on Jesus as Forgiving Victim," an interview in *The Christian Century*, September 5, 2006, http://www.christiancentury.org/article.lasso?id=2331.
2. James Alison, *Raising Abel* (New York: Crossroad, 2003), 29.
3. Alison, "Violence Undone."

Chapter 17: Reverse Glory

1. Fyodor Dostoyevsky, *The Brothers Karamazov* (New York: Signet Classics, 1980), 265.
2. James Alison, "Violence Undone: James Alison on Jesus as Forgiving Victim," an interview in *The Christian Century*, September 5, 2006, http://www.christiancentury.org/article.lasso?id=2331.

Chapter 18: Delight in the Fatness and Live

1. William Stringfellow, *My People Is the Enemy* (New York: Doubleday Anchor, 1964), 102.
2. Ibid., 100.